Essentials has emerged out of the very life that the author, Kim Kerr, has been living and experiencing. The women portrayed in this book speak louder than ever to the women of our times. *Essentials* will help ground our thinking and practice in the Word of God. A must-read book to be owned and treasured by women across the globe who love the Lord Jesus Christ and want to follow Him wholeheartedly.
—**Koki Desai**, Retired Women's Director, Evangelical Fellowship of India, WiW Regional Associate India

Essentials brings the Bible to life through a feminine lens, equipping women to make a lasting impact on the world around us. —**Shirin Taber**, Executive Producer, Empower Women Media

Kim Kerr combines humility with dignity, gentleness with firmness, simplicity with sharpness. She poured all this into her book as she has been pouring into women's lives across nations and cultures. I am definitely one of these women! In her book, she takes us back to the "essentials" God had envisioned for our lives. —**Nada Safi Haddad**, Women's Ministry Director, Near East Organization, Beirut, Lebanon

In this age, women have become overwhelmed with responsibilities of work, ministry, home, family, kids, not to mention finances and safety. This book takes us back to the **essentials** of life that we tend to overlook. I recommend it to every woman searching for a simple yet deep and fruitful way to study the Bible and reflect on her life through it! —**Christelle Boustany Al Khazen**, Trainer and Coordinator, Near East Organization, Beirut, Lebanon

I recommend this book because women not only need to know how to read the Bible, but to find themselves between the lines. The practical tips and points of *Essentials* help us to easily apply the life lessons and learn from the role models of women in God's Word. *Essentials* Bible Study provides a way to be self-led to understand and grow in faith. It includes both a self-learning process and a group-learning process. These easy tips of discovering the message will lead us to pursue a joyful Journey as women from different countries unite around the One Divine Story. —**Basma Gammoh**, Program Manager and Trainer, *Arab Woman Today*

Essentials is a book I recommend. Every woman around the world should have it with her right next to her Bible! I would say it should be translated into many languages! I have never learnt a simpler way to study and understand the Bible as the method of the inductive narrative Bible Study. This method helped a lot women in church to love to read and study the Bible! —**Karima Chalah**, Leader of the "Woman to Woman" Ministry, Church of Tizi-ouzou, Algeria

Kim Kerr's *Essentials* so beautifully draws our eyes upward to Christ, our one true Essential, reminding us of the joy and freedom that comes from knowing we are part of His redemptive work in the world. Kim Kerr then guides our vision outward, teaching us to see all the ways God is working in and through women across the globe, despite many difficult circumstances. *Essentials* clearly shows us that God has a good and beautiful plan for us as women, and it is an honor to be created in His image and for His glory. This is a necessary book for women, leading us to discover our great God and the role we play in His great story. —**Sarah Pascual**, Executive Director, Resonate Church Atlanta

In her book *Essentials*, Kim Kerr presents a compilation of years of study and practical application, a deep knowledge of the Bible, and her heart for women around the world. Whether used individually or within a group setting, *Essentials* presents a theologically sound method of observation, interpretation, and application of Scripture. Based on the unchanging Word of God and the stories of real women, it reveals how God's work in and through women crosses the   'tal status. It is a beautiful reminder that God continues to be at work i   rs, we are invited to study His Word, to correctly analyze and accurat   othy 2:15), and to share that Truth with others (2 Timothy 2:2). ·   stance Learning Professor

D1379369

What a great idea for a book at this time: exploring biblical essentials for a fulfilling life. Kim writes with warmth and authority based on Bible truth and also grounded in her long experience of training and encouraging women in many different cultures. Grab a copy to read alone or with a study group.
—**Amanda Jackson**, Executive Director, Women's Commission of the World Evangelical Alliance

Essentials

DISCOVER THE ESSENTIALS FOR A
MEANINGFUL LIFE AND ETERNAL LEGACY

(A narrative inductive Bible study)

You are an Essential part of God's Story!

Kim Kerr
Founding Director
Women in the Window International, Inc.

Blessings in Christ,

Kim

GROUND TRUTH PRESS
NASHUA, NEW HAMPSHIRE

Essentials:

Discover the Essentials for a Meaningful Life and Eternal Legacy

Published by GROUND TRUTH PRESS
P. O. Box 7313
Nashua, NH 03060-7313

Copy Editor: Bonnie Lyn Smith

Cover Design: Jay Adcock, Adcock Creative Group
Cover and Title Page Art: Cienpies Design/Shutterstock.com

Graphic Design: Susannah Welch
Author Photographer: Andrea Graeve | Photography & Design
Credits for interior photographs used by permission are listed at the end of this book.
All other photos belong to the author.

Icons made by Pixel perfect from www.flaticon.com.

First printing 2020
Printed in the United States of America

Women in the Window Narrative Inductive Bible Study (© 2020 Kim Kerr)

Scripture quotations marked (NASB), the most prevalent within the book, are taken from The Hebrew-Greek Key Study Bible: New American Standard Bible, Copyright © 1994 by AMG Publishers. Used by permission. All rights reserved.

Scripture quotations marked (AMP) are taken from the Amplified Bible, Copyright © 1954, 1958, 1962, 1964, 1965, 1987 by The Lockman Foundation. Used by permission.

Scripture quotations marked (CSB) are taken from the Christian Standard Bible. Copyright © 2017 by Holman Bible Publishers. Used by permission. Christian Standard Bible®, and CSB® are federally registered trademarks of Holman Bible Publishers, all rights reserved.

Scripture quotations marked (ESV) are taken from the ESV® Bible (The Holy Bible, English Standard Version®), copyright © 2001 by Crossway, a publishing ministry of Good News Publishers. Used by permission. All rights reserved.

Scripture quotations marked (MSG) are taken from *THE MESSAGE*, copyright © 1993, 2002, 2018 by Eugene H. Peterson. Used by permission of NavPress. All rights reserved. Represented by Tyndale House Publishers, Inc.

Scripture quotations marked (NIV) are taken from the Holy Bible, New International Version®, NIV®. Copyright © 1973, 1978, 1984, 2011 by Biblica, Inc.® Used by permission of Zondervan. All rights reserved worldwide. www.zondervan.com The "NIV" and "New International Version" are trademarks registered in the United States Patent and Trademark Office by Biblica, Inc.®

Scripture quotations marked (NJKV) are taken from taken from the New King James Version®. Copyright © 1982 by Thomas Nelson. Used by permission. All rights reserved.

Scripture quotations marked (NLT) are taken from the *Holy Bible*, New Living Translation, copyright © 1996, 2004, 2015 by Tyndale House Foundation. Used by permission of Tyndale House Publishers, Inc., Carol Stream, Illinois 60188. All rights reserved.

Trade paperback ISBN-13: 978-1-7359307-1-8
Trade paperback ISBN-10: 1735930717

DEDICATION

To my seven granddaughters:

Bella Kristina
Madeline Rose
Jada Marleasa
Tatianna Machelle
Claire Lane
Kalyah Maria
Emilia Iris

Like the seven beautifully carved pillars of the palace in Proverbs 9:1-2, stand strong. Discover the essentials for your meaningful lives, found only in God's Word, and your unique, eternal legacy woven into the tapestry of Christ's Redeeming Grace.

I love you so,
Mimi

Do not fear, for I am with you;
I will bring your offspring from the east,
And gather you from the west.
I will say to the north, "Give *them* up!"
And to the south, "Do not hold *them* back."
Bring My sons from afar
And My daughters from the ends of the earth.

Isaiah 43:5-6 NASB

Each purchase of this book makes it possible for women in Africa, Asia and the Middle East to receive a free copy of *Essentials*. Thank you for helping Women in the Window International share the teaching of God's Word to the very ends of the earth!

CONTENTS

Prologue: Essentials in a Time of Crisis i

1 Those Amazing Women 1

2 Essentials for a Woman's Life 7

3 How to Get the Most Out of This Bible Study 13

4 Relationships That Matter 25

5 Beauty That Lasts 45

6 Education That Has an Impact 63

7 Fertility and Motherhood 83

8 Creativity That Leads to Generosity 101

Conclusion: His Essential Love for You 121

Epilogue: One Thing Only Is Essential 123

Photo Credits 125

Acknowledgments 127

About the Author 129

About Women in the Window International 130

PROLOGUE
Essentials in a Time of Crisis

W E WILL ALWAYS remember the coronavirus (COVID-19) season and its impact on our lives, our economy, and our world. It was the first time in history that the entire world stood still—paying attention to a virus, as it became a global pandemic, that swept through every nation across the world.

Never in the history of mankind had there been anything that commanded the attention of the leadership and the citizens of every nation, culture, and generation in quite the same way that COVID-19 did. Never before did the people around the world have the technology to connect and communicate in real time. While more than one million lives have been lost at the time of this writing, *every* life was altered as we were told to *shelter in place.*

We were told to only do what was ***essential*** to our well-being. Grocery store shelves were empty, and here in the United States, toilet paper seemingly became our most treasured possession. Workers were laid off and, in many cases, only essential jobs remained. The stock market dropped, and then dropped some more. Despair and even depression loomed. Uncertainty became, well, certain.

When will this end? How will it end? What will the future hold? These became some of the essential questions that we pondered and discussed. And for those of us who pray? We prayed for God's mercy. Oh, how we prayed! His help became our greatest essential.

In this context, the word ***essential*** takes on a clear meaning: **vital, indispensable, important, crucial, critical, and necessary.**[1] That which is essential is precious. It can be life-giving and hope-producing. In the very midst of this time of extraordinary uncertainty, one thing is certain—God and His Word. His Word is the clearest expression of His character revealed this side of Heaven. The Word of God is Life-giving, creative. God literally speaks to us through His Word.

---

[1] "Essential: Synonyms of Essential by Oxford Dictionary on Lexico.com. Also Antonyms of Essential," accessed October 18, 2020, https://www.lexico.com/synonym/essential.

And, the Word comes to us in various forms, such as poetry, prose, prophecy, preaching, and stories or narrative. We will explore this more fully in the chapters to come, but for now, meditate on the beautiful reality that God is literally in His Word:

In the beginning was the Word, and the Word was with God, and the Word was God. He was with God in the beginning. Through him all things were made; without him nothing was made that has been made. In him was life, and that life was the light of all mankind. John 1:1-4 NIV

Yes! God is in His Word. His Word proceeds from His heart to express His truth and love. In this passage, the "Word" refers to Jesus. The Bible reveals to us that Jesus is the Son of God, equal to God the Father and God the Holy Spirit. He is the Author of Life and Light, and He freely offers both to all of mankind. Did you catch that? *All* of mankind. He is our **one true essential**. His Word reveals this truth in beautiful and transformative ways.

That's why this Bible study is called *Essentials*. There is absolutely nothing more essential for our lives, relationships, and future hope. When we finally understand just how essential His Word truly is, we become like those very first Christians in the book of Acts. Although they were told to be quiet and stop talking about Him, they simply, humbly replied, **"… we cannot stop speaking about what we have seen and heard"** (Acts 4:20 NASB).

My Essentials Story

The truth of the matter is that I simply cannot stop talking about God either. He *is* my essential!

You see, He saved my soul, rescuing me from my own foolish trajectory. As much as I wanted to do the right things, they never turned out right. I can fully identify with Romans 7:15 (NIV): **"I do not understand what I do. For what I want to do I do not do, but what I hate I do."** The more I tried to do the right things, the more I simply could not pull it off. I continued to slip into the patterns of behavior that were reflective of the unbelieving world and pleasing to the flesh. I needed to see for myself that this world, my flesh, and the devil himself was at war with what I *really* wanted. All that I really needed, my *essentials*, were found in Christ alone. He heard the cries of my heart even before I knew how to put them to words. He was preparing my heart to sing a new song—a song of love and joy.

Yes! Somehow, God in His wonder and mercy, reached down to rescue me. He is the God who sees, saves, and places incredible value on the soul of each person He has created. When I finally understood that, or I should say, when He made it clear to me, everything changed. And I do mean *everything*! It was as if each leaf on every tree was singing a love song to me—a love song that enabled me to feel the love of our Savior and to be transformed from the inside out.

> **He brought me up out of the pit of destruction, out of the miry clay…He put a new song in my mouth, a song of praise to our God; many will see and fear and will trust in the LORD.** Ps. 40:2-3 NASB

I had only just begun to live and had so much to learn (I still do). This learning journey led to a whole new depth, breadth, and height of living a life of freedom in Christ as His death on the cross set me free from the power sin held over my life.

The Bible is intended to help each one of us live more fully and freely. We are free to be who we truly are and to enjoy our unique, God-given purpose in this world as we grow in understanding. His Word captivates and liberates all at the same time, giving us the power we need to resist and overcome temptation. It grants us the strength so often needed to overcome trials and sorrows, replacing them with joy. He says, **"If you abide in my Word, then you are truly my disciples, and you will know the truth, and the truth will set you free"** John 8:31b-32 (ESV).

It's been thousands of years since that Word was written, and decades since it set me free. Yet its strength and liberating purpose has not changed or diminished at all. In fact, in this age of globalization we can clearly see that it is more essential than ever before. More than ever, we need to know and live in Truth. Truth sets us free from the daunting challenges of our own culture and generation. And isn't it wonderful to recognize that God's Word and Truth, and yes, His love, too is the same yesterday, today and will be forever?

Yes, Jesus and His Word are *essential* to me. My prayer is that this unique approach to Bible study will make Him become even more precious and essential for you, too. I'm thrilled to invite you on this journey with me, to explore the lives of women in the window of God's Word and discover the essentials for a meaningful life. First let's determine together just how to leave an eternal legacy as we connect women across cultures and generations—to treasure and proclaim His Good News:

> **The Lord announces the word,**
> **and the women who proclaim it are a mighty throng.**
> Ps. 68:11 NIV

1
THOSE AMAZING WOMEN

Y EP, THAT'S WHAT the men said!

> **But also some women among us *amazed us*. When they were at the tomb early in the morning, and did not find His body, they came, saying that they had also seen a vision of angels, who said that He was alive. And some of those who were with us went to the tomb and found it just *exactly* as the women also had said....** (Luke 24:22-24 NASB)

Do you remember the story of the two disciples walking along the Emmaus Road with Jesus? They gave Him a detailed recount of all that had just taken place in Jerusalem, including His own crucifixion. Heartsick and forlorn, they were amazed by these women who offered them a ray of hope. God wants all of us to be amazing women who clarify the situation at hand, call others to action, and offer hope through our God and His story!

The people who know God personally will be strong and take action, according to Daniel 11:32b. These people of strength include men and women—even boys and girls. The idea that women and girls are among this number does not seem exceptional to many of us living in the twenty-first century. But the truth is that even today, life is incredibly difficult for many women and girls. In many local communities, they are worth less than the livestock they feed and milk. Their worth may be continually in question and their safety of no real concern. Even so, God calls them His *beloved* and welcomes them into His Kingdom to become known and honored as faithful, fruitful—and yes—amazing!

What makes them amazing?

Simple answer: Jesus's Presence with them and His Power upon them.

Although the answer is simple, the path for women to know Jesus may not be. For the majority of women and girls in the world, the path to Jesus proves a difficult climb. Poverty severely limits their access to biblical teaching. Persecution and oppression can make the journey towards Christ a treacherous one.

Yet, women are an essential part of God's Story. His story was and is incomplete without them, as we discover in the very first book of the Bible: "It is not good for man to be alone" (Gen. 2:18). And *we* are essential in the larger Story of redemption. God's purposes include women to bring about the redemption of all mankind.

Herbert Lockyer, author of *All the Women of the Bible*, has this to say:

> A continuous sojourn for over a year in the world of Bible women, caused one to realize how intimately they were associated with the unfolding purpose of God. With the first woman He fashioned there came the first promise and prophecy of His redemptive plan for mankind. Because He is no respecter of person or sex, He used—and still uses—women to accomplish His beneficent ministry in a world of need. While it is sadly true that it was a woman who brought sin into God's fair universe, it was likewise a woman who gave the world the Saviour from its sin. Furthermore, the student of Scripture female biography is impressed with the fact that men and nations are influenced by the quality of women; and it is still true that "the hand that rocks the cradle rules the world."[2]

Insight from these stories is essential to our growth in Christ and helps us fulfill our highest potential, which includes:

1. Becoming disciples who actively make disciples (Matt. 28:18-20; Acts 1:8)
2. Overcoming cultural, religious, and economic oppression of women and girls (Prov. 31:8-9)
3. Accurately interpreting and diligently applying the transformational Word of God to our lives and situations (2 Tim. 2:15)

So how do we fulfill our potential and extend the Great Commission of Christ in making disciples of all nations, including women? What steps can we take to enable women of all cultures and generations to enter the Kingdom of God as His faithful disciples, who will in turn make more disciples?

I am convinced that the book you are holding has the key.

It is profound yet simple.

Like the women who followed Jesus from the cross to the empty tomb, women across the world are eager to both know God's Truth and to make His Truth known across cultures and generations. With inspiring faith and undaunted courage,

---

[2] Herbert Lockyer, *All the Women of the Bible: The Life and Times of All the Women of the Bible* (Grand Rapids, MI: Zondervan Pub. House, 1995), introduction.

they overcome obstacles and face down opposition. The tools found in this book can help each and every one of us to do just that!

How do I know? I've seen it time and time again. Women in our organization have taught the Women in the Window narrative inductive Bible study (© 2020 Kim Kerr) in dozens of nations to hundreds of women. And each time we do, the result is the same. When women understand they are included in His story and that their stories matter to God, their hearts are deeply stirred, and their lives are transformed. God's Word transforms us from the inside out. Word-by-word, page-by-page, and story-by-story, it enables us to become women and girls of dignity and strength.

God's Word energizes us so that we run in the path of His commandments as our hearts are set free (Ps. 119:32). One of the very best ways to do that is through the study of stories of women in God's infallible and powerful Word. They help us to grasp our ability as females to make a difference within our families, communities, and nations like Miriam and Tabitha did, and to see that, like Esther and Priscilla, women can influence on an international scale, bringing joy and honor for God and for others. And now, *Essentials* Bible study takes this to an even higher level to apply God's Word to the lives of women through 5 key topics that are germane to us all.

Follow along as we see how women *connect across cultures and generations* as they take an essential step into His story and discover their own...

Connect Across Cultures

Her dark eyes lit up, her wrinkled face radiant with joy as she exclaimed, "I don't have to act—this is *my* story!" This winsome Thai lady, marked by the years and tears her life had known, experienced the distinct purpose of this narrative inductive Bible study as she saw her own narrative in God's grand love story of redemption. Through the window of observation, she, along with 64 other women of Northeast Thailand's Isaan people group, discovered the facts of the story of the Samaritan woman found in John 4. Through the window of interpretation, they uncovered the Author's purpose for including this account in the Gospel of John in the Word of God. In that divine moment, through the application window, she relived God's purpose through the dramatization of His principles by a Samaritan evangelist. God has always included women in His story and has a unique role for women that can only be completed as we, His daughters, see ourselves in His story and discover our dignity through His eyes.

This is the story of how Women in the Window Bible study emerged, as the Isaan women of Northeast Thailand laughed, cried, danced, and sang about God's love for all women, evidenced in the pages of His Holy Word—and written indelibly and eternally on their hearts via this interactive Bible study. From this starting point in November 2002, the Women in the Window Bible study has been taught to hundreds of indigenous women leaders in dozens of nations—and they are teaching it to potentially thousands more.

In recent years, however, it has become apparent that this Bible study is a vital tool for reaching and teaching the next generation. The United States has become increasingly secular. Other nations, such as India, with a long history of Christian mission presence have now closed their borders to Christian ministry. And still other nations, such as Algeria, are nailing their church doors shut. We need to train the next generation in ways that are biblically sound and culturally relevant.

Teaching the stories of women from God's ancient, yet timely, Word creates an apologetic approach that is winsome and transformative.

Connect Across Generations

The Bible is clear. God wants us to pass on our faith to the next generation—to connect across cultures as described in Psalm 78:6-7 (NASB):

> …that the generation to come might know, even the children yet to be born, that they may arise and tell them to their children, that they should put their confidence in God, and not forget the works of God, but keep His commandments.

And if we don't, the alternative is not only secularization, but also Islamization and Hinduization. In terms of a Christian presence in the world, that's a grim picture.

An apt illustration of how this may be so can be seen in an aspen forest of Utah. I first learned about this forest from *Today in the Word*, a Moody Global Ministries Devotional. This forest of quaking aspens in Utah is known by the name

"Pando," meaning, "I spread." It's also called the "Trembling Giant." In essence, this forest is a single tree with 40,000 trunks, each of which appears to be a separate tree from an above-ground perspective. But, according to *Smithsonian Magazine*, Pando, one of the world's largest living organisms, is dying:

> Their findings were pretty grim. In most areas of the grove, there are no "young or middle-aged trees at all," lead study author Paul Rogers, an ecologist at Utah State University, tells Yasemin Saplakoglu of *Live Science*. Pando, he adds, is made up almost entirely of "very elderly senior citizens." Conservationists are working on viable methods of protecting and propagating future growth for Pando.[3]

Pando is dying because it is no longer producing younger trees for future growth. As predators of Pando, namely, the deer in the area devour young plants before they have a chance to mature. As women who love and follow Christ as our Savior and Lord, let's learn the example of Pando and impart the powerful and effective tools of narrative inductive Bible study to the next generation. Let's inspire them to live a life of purpose and experience the fulfillment of its promises.

For the promise is for you and your children, and for all who are far off, as many as the Lord our God shall call to Himself. Acts 2:39 NASB

The next generation has their own amazing stories to tell—and to live! Consider Rhoda, a young servant-girl living in the home of Mary, the mother of John Mark who wrote the Gospel of Mark:

> **And they said to her [Rhoda], "you are out of your mind!" But she kept insisting that it was so. And they kept saying, "It is his angel." But Peter continued knocking; and when they opened the door, they saw him and *were amazed.*** Acts 12:15-16 NASB

Just ask Loren Cunningham, founder of YWAM (Youth With A Mission) and co-author of *Why Not Women*:

> As we release women, we'll mobilize the hundreds of thousands of people needed to complete the Great Commission. We'll see God's blessing on unity and servant leadership. We'll see more anointing of the Spirit. We'll see a strong Body of Christ, no longer weakened because we fail to discern it.[4]

Yes! Young and old, from generation to generation, and across every tribe, tongue, nation, and culture in the world—women and girls are amazing!

---

[3] Brigit Katz, "Pando, One of the World's Largest Organisms, Is Dying," October 18, 2018, https://www.smithsonianmag.com/smart-news/pano-one-worlds-largest-organisms-dying-180970579/.
[4] Loren Cunningham and David Joel Hamilton, *Why Not Women? A Fresh Look at Scripture on Women in Missions, Ministry, and Leadership* (Seattle: YWAM Publishing, 2000), 237.

2
ESSENTIALS FOR A WOMAN'S LIFE

"E SSENTIAL" WARDROBES HAVE become quite vogue in recent years.

Websites and specialty shops feature a personalized, *essential* wardrobe to prepare each woman for every opportunity. They include elements such as clothing, shoes, and a few accessories. The interchangeable slacks, skirts, blouses, and more, make getting ready for any occasion seamless. Just grab a few essentials—and off you go!

How much more, then, do we need to focus on the essentials of the *inner* person—our very soul! These *essentials* are quite different. They are invisible. We can't view values, virtues, and qualities like love, joy, peace, or diligence in quite the same way as we can see the material items of our wardrobe. It's not immediately apparent if someone has a lying, backbiting tongue or a jealous spirit. Yet, after a few encounters and conversations, the *essentials* of our soul—**who we are**—readily appear, and eventually, they influence every relationship that we have and inform every decision that we make. Inevitably, they will impact each aspect of life and our eternal legacy.

> **Just what is essential?**
>
> The thesaurus offers these synonyms:
>
> vital, indispensable, important, crucial, critical, necessary

Yes, what really matters most is not the external but the *internal* person of the heart. And while there is not a shop-on-line website where we can purchase the essentials that our soul needs, there is something even better—the Word of God, the Bible.

> **For the word of God is living and active and sharper than any two-edged sword, and piercing as far as the division of soul and spirit, of both joints and marrow, and able to judge the thoughts and intentions of the heart.**
> Heb. 4:12 NASB

This Bible study, *Essentials*, is written to help us focus on what matters most. It should not be a surprise that the God who made us, has the answers we need for each area of life. Yet, we often do not go to Him first. We forget, or maybe never really knew, just how much He loves us—how very deep His compassion is for us. Listen to this:

> **Never! Can a mother forget her nursing child?**
> **Can she feel no love for the child she has borne?**
> **But even if that were possible, I would not forget you!**
> **See, I have written your name on the palms of my hands.**
> Isa. 49:15-16a NLT

This God who made us loves us dearly! We are His greatest treasure. He gave His only Son, Jesus the Christ (the Messiah), to become our Savior and to grant us free access into His Presence day and night—night and day. There is nothing too difficult for Him, and nothing beyond His care or ability to do on our behalf. He never forgets us. His palms are forever etched with the nail prints reminding us that He gave His life for you and for me, too.

What matters most to God are these *essentials*: our soul, or inner person of the heart. Why? Because God knows that as we focus on heart issues, we become beautiful from the inside out. We are then equipped to live a life that is deeply fulfilling to us and helpful to others. With these essentials, we have everything we need to face life's situations with strength and dignity, hope and courage—**all** that is essential.

Life Essentials

In preparation for this Bible study, I asked women to identify the essential areas of their lives: that which matters most to them today as well as their hopes for the future regardless of their background, generation, or culture. Is it any surprise that the women in the Bible grappled with these very same essentials?

The top 5 essentials identified by women across the world today and displayed through specific women in the Bible, include:

- Relationships that matter—Priscilla
- Beauty that lasts—Esther
- Education that has an impact—Huldah
- Fertility and motherhood—Hannah
- Creativity that leads to generosity—Lydia

Without God's help, we tend to have a short-term perspective that settles for less than the best. If we only evaluate what *seems* right in the here and now, we shortchange ourselves. God wants to help us make decisions that we will not regret. He makes the path straight before us when we lean on Him and not on our own understanding. Not only do we make better decisions with Him at our sides, but we also become better people. We become women who are beautiful from the inside out—a beauty that attracts others to us and to our God.

God cares deeply for us and about what is important to each of us. He understands our need to make wise daily and long-term decisions. Even so, learning how to do so is not as easy as shopping for a new wardrobe. In fact, it can be downright daunting. We need the help only God and His Word provides in these essential areas of life.

Why Narrative?

This Bible study is for *every* woman, of every culture and generation. As we explore the essentials in the lives of women in the Bible, we gain incredible insight into our own life—both the blessings we enjoy and the challenges we face. The narratives of women in the Bible illustrate for us how deeply God cares and how attentive He is to the cries of our heart. Through His comfort, we in turn are prepared to offer comfort to others in need:

> **Blessed be the God and Father of our Lord Jesus Christ, the Father of mercies and God of all comfort; who comforts us in all our affliction so that we may be able to comfort those who are in any affliction with the comfort with which we ourselves are comforted by God.** 2 Cor. 1:3-4 ESV

This Bible study is based on the narratives, or stories, about women in the Bible. And there is no shortage—there are more than 100 stories of women included in God's Word.[5] Did you know that approximately one-half of the Bible is written in narrative format? God knows that we remember and apply stories much more readily than we learn facts and figures. In fact, scientists researching educational methods have discovered that **our brains are hard-wired to remember, and then repeat, stories** beyond what we can do with any other source of information. Consider this fascinating fact:

> Something surprising happens when information comes from a story rather than just simple facts: More of our brains light up. When we hear a story, the neural activity increases fivefold, like a switchboard has suddenly illuminated the city of our mind. Scientists have a saying: "Neurons that fire together, wire together." When more of your brain is at work at a given point of time, the chances that your brain will remember the work it did increase exponentially.[6]

---

[5] Visit **www.womeninthewindow-intl.org/essentials** to learn more.

[6] Joe Lazauskas and Shane Snow, "The Strange Thing That Happens In Your Brain When You Hear a Good Story -- And How to Use It to Your Advantage," accessed October 8, 2020. https://blog.hubspot.com/marketing/the-strange-thing-that-happens-in-you-brain-when-you-hear-a-good-story-and-how-to-use-it-to-your-advantage.

Why Inductive?

Essentials is also an inductive Bible study. What exactly does that mean? It means that we will examine precisely what the Word of God says in its original context through the "windows" of **Preparation, Observation, Interpretation, Application, and Reflection:**

- **Preparation** is essential. Would you attempt anything that matters without adequate preparation? Of course not. Read, research, and remember to pray, as you properly prepare to lead this Bible study for others or just yourself.
- **Observation** enables us to clearly see who is in the story, where they were, when this story took place, and what other facts are essential through probing questions.
- **Interpretation** enables us to take these facts and, with the help of the Holy Spirit, discover timeless truth for all people, in all places, and at all times!
- **Application** enables us to take the timeless truth, or eternal essentials of God's Word, and apply them to the daily essentials of our lives in the here and now.
- **Reflection** provides a place and space for our soul to more fully receive the essence of God's character taught through His Word. Just like cleaning our windows expands our view, reflection enables us to clean the windows of our soul through reflective worship.

As we inductively study the stories of women in the Bible, we see that their needs are always met—but not always as expected. I like to say that God always answers prayer, but He often answers it *later*, and *far better* than we could have hoped or imagined! The wonder of God's answers fills our hearts with joy even though the journey to these answers often includes many challenges. The psalmist passionately cried out to God:

> **Answer me when I call, O God of my righteousness!** *Thou hast relieved me in my distress; be gracious to me and hear my prayer. . .* **Thou hast put gladness in my heart, more than when their grain and new wine abound. In peace I will both lie down and sleep, for Thou alone, O LORD, dost make me to dwell in safety"** Ps. 4:1, 7-8 NASB

We will see how each woman's challenges and distress enable them to further grow into in their God-given passions and purposes, as they develop essential character qualities like **integrity, dignity, compassion, trust,** and **ingenuity.**

Their stories are harrowing and heartwarming. The plots twist and turn in unexpected ways. Not at all like a Hallmark movie (no offense to Hallmark movie lovers!), the Bible includes the good, the bad, and yes—the ugly. In biblical narratives, we see ourselves as we really are.

Yet, like a good plastic surgeon, the Holy Spirit enables us to be transformed into who we want to be as the mirror of His Word literally transforms us, bit by bit, right before our very eyes. The Holy Spirit is co-equal with God and the fulfillment of Christ's prayer for us to receive both comfort and companionship when He returned to Heaven after His Resurrection. He gently leads us into all truth:

> **"And I will ask the Father, and He will give you another Helper, that He may be with you forever; that is the Spirit of truth...."** John 14:16-17a NASB

The transformation He provides is nothing less than looking into a well-lit and magnified mirror:

> **And we all, with unveiled face, *continually* seeing as in a mirror the glory of the Lord, are *progressively* being transformed into His image from [one degree of] glory to [even more] glory, which comes from the Lord, [who is] the Spirit.** 2 Cor. 3:18 AMP

As we learn how to study these stories inductively, we find the answers we are looking for and the purpose we are longing for. It's as if God is hand-picking a new wardrobe, custom-made for each one of us.

A New Wardrobe

Now you're dressed in a new wardrobe. Every item of your new way of life is custom-made by the Creator, with His label on it. So, chosen by God for this new life of love, dress in the wardrobe God picked out for you: compassion, kindness, humility, quiet strength, discipline. Be even-tempered, content with second place, quick to forgive an offense. Forgive as quickly and completely as the Master forgave you. And regardless of what else you put on, wear love. it's your basic all-purpose garment. Never be without it. Col. 3:10, 12-14 MSG

Did you catch that? A custom-made and personalized wardrobe by our Creator that makes us beautiful from the inside out. Now that's a shopping spree that I hope you will take with me!

As we see the way God includes and elevates women in the Bible, we will gain both insight and strength for our own personal journeys. As we take a step into His story, we will certainly discover our own story unfolding before our very eyes. We will learn how to discover and even display the beauty and dignity of this priceless wardrobe that never wears out or goes out of style. Uniquely, and in community, we gain the knowledge, wisdom, and understanding to discover and develop the *essentials* for a meaningful life and an eternal legacy.

3
HOW TO GET THE MOST OUT OF
THIS BIBLE STUDY

*E*SSENTIALS BIBLE STUDY teaches how to explore the more than 100 stories of women throughout the Bible, starting with 5 unique women. This chapter teaches us **"How To"** effectively use this Bible study method as an individual or group leader.

Get ready to thoroughly investigate and then delightfully discover relevant truths found in God's Word as we celebrate the power of His Word, the incredible value of women, and the life-changing impact of their stories. As we look to the examples of Priscilla, Esther, Huldah, Hannah, and Lydia in the Bible, we come to better understand our own story. We see glimpses of ourselves and learn essential lessons about what we need to embrace, avoid, and correct.

Begin with the biblical overview of the essential topics of relationships, beauty, education, fertility and motherhood, and creativity, as we learn to evaluate life's choices through the lens of God's Word. While there are no blueprints for our journey through life, there is a roadmap of truth and a pathway of love set before us by the Lover of our souls, Jesus Christ.

Preparation is a must. We don't begin anything worthwhile without preparation, do we? In this Bible study, I have researched and included the background for each story.

Proceed to the three steps of inductive Bible study: **Observation, Interpretation, and Application**. *Essentials* includes worksheets for each participant, including you, as well as an example of Interpretation, which is often the most challenging part of this process. Only the *Essentials* study of Beauty, as seen in the life of Esther, requires two weeks for a group study, but the nuggets of truth within that study are well worth the investment of time. Each chapter concludes with **Reflection** to renew and refresh our souls.

How to Study and Teach *Essentials*

This Bible study was designed for individual and/or group study. Each chapter of *Essentials* will include five inductive Bible study steps.[7] *If studying as a group*, the group leader provides an overview of Preparation during the first session that leads into both Observation and Interpretation of the Scripture. Application is discussed, and then each participant has seven distinct points to ponder for the seven days that follow. The second session includes a lively group Application. So much fun! Reflection provides a way for each participant, including you, to grow deeper in God's Word as His Holy Spirit refreshes and renews your soul.

The following is a Recommended Group Schedule:

- Each class will range from 60 to 90 minutes, depending upon your group.
- Only "Beauty," the study of Esther, will require two full weeks/sessions.
- We estimate that you can complete the entire *Essentials* Bible study in six or seven weeks.

You will recognize each step of your *Essentials* Bible study journey when you see the following symbols:

 Preparation—Consider the context.

 Observation—Collect the facts.

 Interpretation—Compile the truths.

 Application—Walk it out; put the truth into practice.

 Reflection—Clean the window to our souls through reflective worship.

---

[7] Visit **www.womeninthewindow-intl.org/essentials** to download the *Essentials* infographic and worksheets.

 Preparation

Even as we prepare for a scrumptious recipe, we need to gather our ingredients, consider the temperature, and then proceed. In much the same way, we prepare as we read, research, and always remember to pray.

Read her story in an **essentially literal Bible translation** (such as the New American Standard Bible or English Standard Version), which translates the Bible word for word, and in a **dynamic equivalent version** (such as the New Living Translation or New International Version), which translates thought for thought. Read it thoroughly *before* consulting commentaries, Bible dictionaries, or other Bible study resources. Whenever possible, read out loud and more than once.

Research the background of the story to determine context and type of literature, and to understand the writer's aim for the original audience. To get you started, I have shared some of my own research for each of the five essentials. And the following questions will you help you both study and teach *Essentials.* **Ask and answer** the following questions about context:

1. *Where do we find this woman's (or women) story in the Bible?* The Old or New Testament? *What type of literature or genre of the Bible is it?* Law, history, prophecy, poetry, the Gospel narrative, or an epistle?

   The **type of literature or genre** will affect the way God wants us to interpret the story.[8]

   Example:
   The poetry of Judges 5 is set in contrast to the story of Judges 4, although both chapters tell the story of Deborah. In Judges 4, the facts are recorded as a narrative or story, listing facts in a sequence of events as they unfold. Judges 5, however, includes poetic language such as: "The stars fought from heaven, from their courses they fought against Sisera" (Judges 5:20 NASB). While both versions of Deborah's story are true, they give us an entirely different perspective of how God is at work to save His people and how He includes the story of Deborah, a prophet and judge, to bring about His Kingdom purposes for the redemption of Israel.

2. *How does the **context** inform the meaning of this passage?* Please consider: a) the *immediate context* (passages before and after the passage), b) the *historical, cultural and social context* (circumstances of the audience), c) the *biblical context* (Old or New Testament, references from or historical connections that the author is making and the type of literature or genre).

3. *Who wrote the specific book of the Bible where we find her story?* God is the Author of the Bible, but He carefully chose individuals to pen His Word. It's an important part of our study to examine the writer's life. Based on your background study, examine the **writer's aim** for *his audience* in the context. It is helpful to read the section before and/or after her story to provide more insight into the context.

---

[8] Visit **www.womeninthewindow-intl.org/essentials** to download a helpful Biblical genre tool.

Essentials Preparation Research of each woman's story includes these three preparation questions, but they may not appear in this exact order. Enjoy the creative process of learning from the source of wisdom and Truth, God and His Word:

> **I have not gone back from the commandment of His lips; I have esteemed and treasured up the words of His mouth more than my necessary food.**
> Job 23:12 AMP

<u>**Remember**</u> **the incredible power of prayer.** God has something special to say to you through His Word. While the timeless truths in each story are for everyone, He understands you and your needs, and He wants to meet you right where you are.

Evelyn Christenson, author of *What Happens When Women Pray* and *Lord, Change Me,* spent at least one-third of her Bible study preparation time in prayer. Let's follow Evelyn's example and embrace our opportunity to lead Bible study by praying diligently in preparation. Prayer prepares us and those we teach to fully unlock the treasures of God's Word.

While I did want to provide this brief outline of Bible study Preparation steps for your future use, in each chapter of *Essentials*, the Preparation step has already been done to provide context and clarity, *and* to lead you to the *love and good works* God has planned just for YOU!

> **Let us think of ways to motivate one another to acts of *love and good works.***
> Heb. 10:24 NLT

Observation

Observation answers the question: **"What does it say?"** Read the story; then list the related facts of who, where, when, and what, noting **the verse** or verses where each fact is found. This step is often the most time-consuming yet vital and absolutely worth the effort.

> **Be diligent to present yourself approved to God as a workman who does not need to be ashamed, accurately handling the word of truth.** 2 Tim. 2:15 NASB

Read the story, and if possible, read it two times from different translations of the Bible (word-for-word and thought-for-thought translations). I find it especially helpful to read the story out loud. List the chapter and verse where you find the following:

<u>Who</u> was she?

- What do we see about her in the text?
- List all people included in the story, including all references to God the Father, Jesus Christ, and the Holy Spirit, including pronouns.
- Take special note of repeated words and phrases. There is a reason why things are listed more than once.

<u>Where</u> did she live? worship? work? travel?

- List all **places** in the story, as well as "where" words like *inside, under, behind,* etc.

<u>When</u> did she live?

- List **time-related words** like *before* or *after.*
- Note when this takes place in the Bible and in history.

What other important facts do we learn about her?

What did she do, say, or contribute?

What problem did she create or resolve?

What is the most significant contribution of her life?

What is her essential? Is there a key Bible verse that exemplifies her essential?

List important facts and lessons learned from the story—why do these facts matter? As you observe the key details recorded by answering the questions: **Who, Where, and When,** you will begin to see just why God included them in His Word. As you carefully reassemble your observations from the story by answering the questions referring to **What,** each woman's contribution will become clear and lead you to effective interpretation.

Interpretation

Interpretation asks and answers the question: **"What does the story mean?"** Now that we have accurately observed the facts, we can properly interpret or discern at least two timeless "truths" from this story (there are usually many more than two). A timeless truth from God's Word is true for all people, in all places, and at all times. We discover timeless truths through careful study and by prayerfully applying these general principles of biblical interpretation:

1. **Pray** for wisdom, remembering that the primary purpose of Bible study is to change our lives, not simply to increase our knowledge.

2. **Establish the Bible as *the* authoritative source of Truth,** given to us by God Himself (Heb. 4:12; 2 Tim. 3:16-17; Isa. 40:8).

3. **The Bible interprets itself;** Scripture best explains Scripture. We pay attention to the context of the story, look for cross-references[9] to clarify, recognize repeated words and phrases, and note the genre or type of literature.

4. **Interpret personal experience in the light of Scripture** and *not* Scripture in the light of personal experience. (Syncretism can result from seeing our cultural norms as if they are from God, rather than developing our cultural norms based on God's Word. An example of syncretism is found in Colossians 2:4, as new believers were deluded by the "plausible arguments" of Gnosticism.)

---

[9] Cross-references are other Bible verses in the Old and New Testaments that validate this same truth.

5. **Interpreting a text without context might lead to pretext.** Context clarifies, while pretext confuses and creates error. For example: Biblical examples are authoritative only when supported by a command. Don't make a command from something that is intended as an illustration: Matthew 5:30, **"cut off your right hand."**

Utilizing these principles of interpretation[10], let's discover together at least two examples from God's Word of what is true for all people, in all places, at all times. List the verses where these truths are found. If possible, include a cross-referenced Bible verse that validates this timeless truth.

Timeless Truth #1:

_____

Timeless Truth #2:

_____

 Application

And remember, it is a message to obey, not just to listen to. If you don't obey, you are only fooling yourself. For if you just listen and don't obey it is like looking at your face in a mirror but doing nothing to improve your appearance. You see yourself, walk away, and forget what you look like. But if you keep looking steadily into God's perfect law—and if you do what it says and don't forget what you heard, then God will bless you for doing it. James 1:22-25 NLT

Application answers the question: **"What does this truth mean for me?"** and **"How do I live in response?"** In this step, it is time to apply God's timeless truths to our own lives. The application step helps us to remember truth far more than if we only listened to or spoke the truth. We want to not only *know* what it says but to also *do* what it says!

---

[10] Walter Henrichsen & Gayle Jackson, *Studying, Interpreting, and Applying the Bible* (Grand Rapids: Zondervan, 1990), 147-178.

Gather in small groups, and read the timeless truths you have discovered out loud. Determine which timeless truth is most relevant for the women in your small group. Read and respond to the following questions together as someone in the group records your answers. You may only apply one or two of these questions as you develop an application to share, but review all seven of them as you prepare. This is one of your takeaways; think about one each day of the coming week.

Ask, "Is there a(n) _____?"

1. principle to apply
2. command to obey
3. attitude to change
4. sin to renounce
5. truth to believe
6. example to follow
7. specific action to take

Now, for the fun part! If you are studying this Bible study as an individual, prepare a creative way to remember, and possibly share your timeless truth through poetry, story, drama, other creative artforms, or even as a current events story that relates to today.

If you are studying this as a small group, develop one of the following oral arts to express what you have learned. Together, create a meaningful:
Song,

Dance,

Skit of a modern life drama from your community and nation

Poem recitation, or…

Storytelling—maybe even *your* story!

In *Teaching to Change Lives*, Dr. Howard Hendricks teaches that we generally remember only about 10 percent of what we hear alone, up to 50 percent of what we hear and read, but we have the potential to remember up to 90 percent of what we see, hear, and experience.[11] This Bible Study method helps you to *remember* and *apply* God's Truth to your life—and to multiply that Truth into the lives of other women.

---

[11] Dr. Howard Hendricks, *Teaching to Change Lives, Seven Proven Ways to Make Your Teaching Come Alive* (Sisters, Oregon: Multnomah Press, 1987).

"Psychologists tell us we have the potential of remembering only up to 10 percent of what we hear. And that's potential, not actual. As a matter of fact, if you do remember 10 percent of what you hear, you're in the genius category. Unfortunately, the bulk of Christian education is hearing oriented. That's why it's often so inefficient.

If we add seeing to hearing, psychologist say our potential for remembering goes up to 50 percent…

What about adding doing to seeing and hearing? They psychologists say this combination brings the percentage of memory up to 90 percent—and decades of teaching in a graduate institution have given me all the evidence I need to be convinced that's exactly true."

Each small group will share their application activity with the larger group and will ask the larger group to determine which timeless truth is being displayed. After you complete your application, share further insight about why this timeless truth is essential.

Timeless truth to be presented:

_____

Method selected for presentation (song, dance, story, etc.):

_____

Reflection

We clean the windows of our soul through contemplative, or reflective, spiritual disciplines and practices. What a difference it makes when the windows of my home are clean. The breathtaking view outside is renewing and life-giving. In the same way, as we contemplate the truth(s) we've learned through this narrative inductive Bible study, we can see what is essential to renew, refocus—and yes—_cleanse_ our souls.

Reflection is our final step, and yet it opens the window of our soul to receive the refreshing wind of the Holy Spirit. Engage in an activity that is refreshing for your soul. I like to call this _soul food_. A few of the spiritual practices that you might enjoy as you study individual women, or even groups of women, in the Bible include:

- *Lectio Divina*, or personal meditation on the Word of God
- solitude
- silence
- fasting
- fellowship
- confession
- creativity

As an individual, you might express your own creativity through a creative medium that enables you to process and pray over the spiritual principles you have discovered through a woman in the window of God's Word. And you might include a spiritual discipline such as fasting, prayer, or solitude and silence. An example is just ahead…

Solitude and Silence

Just how does this work? After you have discovered a timeless truth, take some time to reflect on it with the help of the Holy Spirit. Perhaps you are captivated by Mary of Bethany anointing Jesus for His burial with nard that cost her nearly one year's wages. The timeless truth is that **nothing is wasted when we offer it to our Lord**. This may, for example, compel you to think and pray about what you have to offer Him.

Your time of reflection might include a day, or a half-day solitude retreat. Take your Bible, your journal, and a pen. Sit alone in nature or in a special corner of your home as you wait and listen for His voice. I promise—you will *not* be disappointed. Warren Wiersbe describes Mary of Bethany in this way:

> Mary was a deeply spiritual woman. She found at His feet her blessing, brought to His feet her burdens, and gave at His feet her best.[12]

I am convinced that as we spend time "at His feet," we, too, will understand just how our story is truly part of God's global redemption story. Reflection strengthens us from within, and it enables us to know and treasure Him as our highest Essential!

---

[12] Dr. Warren Wiersbe, *The Bible Exposition Commentary, Volume 1 of the New Testament* (Colorado Springs, Colorado: Victor Books, 1989).

How to Get the Most Out of This Bible Study

This **Essentials infographic** is a roadmap of *how to* take an essential step into His story and discover our own. It can be downloaded at **www.womeninthewindow-intl.org/essentials**, along with other helpful resources!

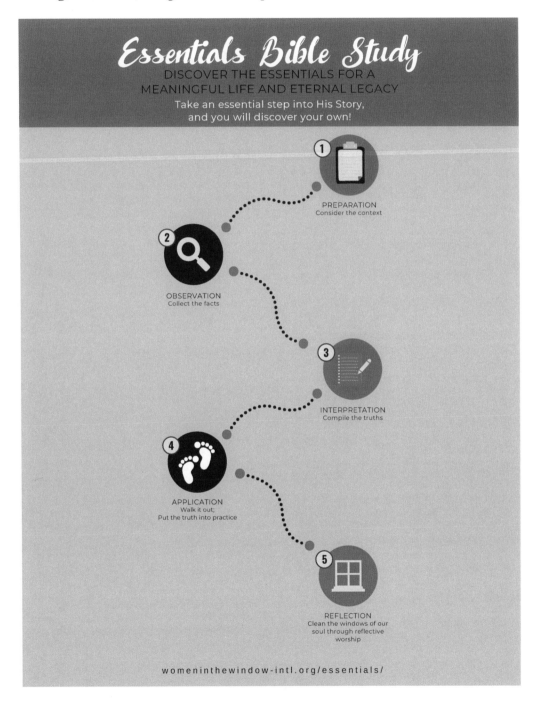

4
RELATIONSHIPS THAT MATTER

FROM ITS VERY first chapter, the Bible clearly reveals God's design for women, with an emphasis on our relationships. Adam was incomplete without Eve. The Story of God was unfinished, and the pinnacle of His creation, man, was impoverished without the rich and beautiful gift of woman. How sad to see that, fairly quickly, this picture of ultimate fulfillment was destroyed from within as both Eve and Adam fell from grace—a fall that would impact every individual, family, community, and nation that followed. The shame and blame cycle began, and the enemy of our souls and our relationships grinned a mocking, evil smirk.

Relationships

God longs for the relationship that He instituted with both the man and the woman, and He calls out to them, *"Where are you?"* The haunting reply from the shadows: *"I was afraid."* You see, Adam and Eve hid from the source of all love, joy, peace, and relationship. Yet God pursued them. Yet God forgave them. Yet God redeemed them.[13]

---

[13] Read the full story in Genesis 3:1-21.

Ruth Haley Barton has this to say about our separation from the Lover of our souls:

> The fallout from this one event included the introduction of sin and guilt, shame and blame, wrongful domination and seduction into male-female relationships. This was in direct contradiction to the oneness, equality, and mutuality that characterized God's best plan for gender relations—which he established in creation and reclaimed through the redeeming work of Christ as Paul summarizes it in Galatians 3:28.[14]

This One who came to reverse the curse also reflects God's heart toward women and men as He teaches us how to live in compatible community. Each time Jesus interacts with a woman in the Bible, we catch a glimpse of God's original intent to honor, include, and empower women, positioning us for significant service. Women become his patrons, his disciples, and some of his dearest friends. Even though Jewish culture often excluded and diminished women, Jesus validated them with both His servant heart toward them and redemptive relationships with them.

Yes, not only does God long for relationship, but we do, too. As women, we tend to be especially motivated by relationships and to prioritize family time and friendships as one of our greatest treasures in life. As we explore the topic of relationship in God's Word, we will view it through the story of Priscilla, who is inextricably bound to her husband Aquila. They are never mentioned apart from one another.

I want to encourage you to delve deeply into the story of Priscilla and to observe the other relationships we see in her life, both her marriage *and* in ministry. She is heralded as a woman of great value by the Apostle Paul and provides an instrumental role in the life of Apollos. Scripture tells us that Apollos was an eloquent and learned man from Alexandria, Egypt. At this point in history, Alexandria was known as a center of learning with a university library containing more than 700,000 volumes. Apollos clearly knew about Christ but stopped short with the baptism of John as the foundation of his teaching. Together with her husband Aquila, Priscilla introduced him to the greatest relationship of all—a saving relationship with Jesus Christ as his Lord and Savior.

Relationships—Do They Matter?

According to God's Word, relationships matter—a lot! Relationships form the picture of the Trinity. The reality of the Trinity, one God in three Divine Persons, is

---

[14] R. Ruth Barton, *Life Together in Christ: Experiencing Transformation in Community* (Downers Grove: IVP Books, an imprint of InterVarsity Press, 2014), 86-87.

referred to throughout the Bible. From this we learn that God is not alone, and that Father, Son and Holy Spirit have perfect harmony and communication.[15]

In much the same way, Priscilla's heart beat as one with her husband, Aquila. They harmoniously labored together in the Lord's service, and they walked as one, for they had mutually agreed to put Christ first.[16]

If married, we can find great fulfillment in a relationship with our husband. One of our highest and holiest purposes is revealed within this relationship (Prov. 31:10-31; Eph. 5:21-33). Priscilla and Aquila were an endearing couple who tirelessly served the work of Christ wherever needed. What an excellent role model for those who want to use their marriage, and their very life, to make an eternal difference for Christ in a modern culture that has largely departed from Him, where people foolishly think that they can somehow discover a meaningful life or eternal legacy on their own.

If single, we can find joy and satisfaction in relationships with extended family, friends, and coworkers. Often, single people have more freedom to explore and appreciate a multitude of relationships in church and community. Travel is simpler, expanding our relational horizon. The Bible talks about singleness by describing our opportunity to enjoy a life of **"undistracted devotion to the Lord"** (1 Cor. 7:35).

In the resurrection account, women were the first at the grave and the last at the cross. Their passion for relationships drove them to the feet of Jesus on more

---

[15] The grace of the Lord Jesus Christ, and the love of God, and the fellowship of the Holy Spirit, be with you all. 2 Cor. 13:14 NASB

[16] Herbert Lockyer, *All the Women of the Bible* (Grand Rapids: Zondervan, no date listed), 121-125.

than one occasion. In fact, He commended a woman, not a man, in this verse: **"Truly I say to you, wherever this gospel is preached in the whole world, what this woman has done will also be spoken of in memory of her"** (Matt. 26:13 NASB).

The prophet Joel promised that the day would come (Joel 2:28-29) when women would serve Christ, side by side, shoulder to shoulder, with men. And Peter's sermon in Acts 2:16-21 proclaims it as a joyful reality. Not only did Priscilla embody the truth of biblical submission to her husband, Aquila, but he likewise submitted to her, recognizing her worth and empowering her in Christ's service. Yes, Aquila was one of the brave men who was not afraid of the impact women could have to transform our world with the message and love of Jesus Christ. Rather, he chose to include and empower his wife with her speaking gifts to serve the Lord and to spread the Good News far and wide. Their marriage reflects the full teaching of Ephesians 5:21-33 and the beautiful mystery of marriage as a picture of the Church.

What can we learn from Priscilla? Whether we are married or single, her lifestyle of servant leadership is one that we should emulate. Scripture teaches us to desire a well-spoken name more than great riches.[17] Paul only spoke of her with glowing words of commendation and listed her name first more often than not. Wouldn't we all want to be heralded throughout eternity as one who is not ashamed of the Gospel of Christ or afraid to take great risks on its behalf? And to be remembered as one who treated the people closest to us, including and especially our husbands, as well as those we meet for the very first time, with the highest respect?

Like a tree firmly planted by streams of water, which yields its fruit in season and has roots growing deep in the fertile soil of God's Word, Priscilla's life brought forth fruit in her time and even more fruit that remains to this very day.[18] Because of her godly example, she continues to bless and serve the church even now through her model of healthy, holy, loving, and life-giving relationships.[19] Only when the last judgment takes place in the "end of days" when Christ returns will the true *bema*, or judgment seat rewards, be granted to this spiritually stalwart sister in Christ.

> Two are better than one because they have a good return for their labor. For if either of them falls, the one will lift up his companion. But woe to the one who falls when there is not another to lift him up.
>
> Ecclesiastes 4:9-10 (NASB)

May God grant you (and me too!) relationships that matter!

---

[17] Prov. 22:1, Eccles. 7:1.

[18] Ps. 1:1-3; Jer. 17:7-8; John 15:1-2, 8, 16.

[19] Frances Vander Velde, *Women of the Bible* (Grand Rapids: Kregel Publications, 1985), 249.

① Preparation

Our first step in this Essentials narrative inductive Bible study is preparation. If you are teaching an *Essentials* Bible study group, or if you are simply studying on your own, here are three simple but vital steps to help you prepare well. Preparation is most definitely an essential. When we prepare a scrumptious recipe, we gather our ingredients, consider the temperature, and then proceed. In much the same way, we prepare for Bible study as we **read, research, and always remember to pray.**

READ her story in an essentially literal Bible translation (word-for-word) such as the English Standard Version and a dynamic equivalent version (thought-for-thought) such as the New Living Translation. Whenever possible, read out loud and more than once.

RESEARCH the background of the story to determine context and the type of literature, and to understand the writer's aim for the original audience. To get you started, I have shared some of my own notes with you below.

REMEMBER TO PRAY—God has something special to say to you through His Word. While the timeless truths in each story are for everyone, He understands you and your needs, and He wants to meet you right where you are. As you pray, you open your heart to receive His personal and practical Word of exhortation and hope.

Read the story of **Priscilla and Aquila** more than once, and read it out loud. There is something very powerful about reading and rereading, the Word of God. Remember, God, says that His Word is alive and that it gives life. It brings light and dispels darkness. It corrects errors and reinforces truth. It replaces fear and anxiety with faith, hope, and love, as we see and hear just how deeply God loves us. If you invest this time in reading and rereading, you will not be disappointed!

> **How sweet are Thy words to my taste! Yes, sweeter than honey to my mouth!**
> Psalm 119:103 NASB

We find the story of Priscilla and Aquila in the following passages:

- Acts 18:1-28
- Romans 16:3-5
- 1 Corinthians 16:19
- 2 Timothy 4:19

Where is her story found, and who wrote it?

My research revealed that Priscilla appears in four different books of the New Testament: the book of Acts, historical narrative written by Luke the physician and historian; and three epistles or letters, all written by the Apostle Paul. The first two of these letters, Romans and 1 Corinthians, are written to specific churches. Second Timothy is considered the last or final book Paul wrote; it was addressed to his son in the faith, Timothy. Reading the first paragraph of this letter, you will immediately note Paul's tender tone towards Timothy. But make no mistake, although it was penned by Paul to Timothy and other Christian believers nearby, it is the infallible and living Word of God, able to instruct us, admonish us, comfort us, and give us life!

We often consider a person's *last* words more weighty than what they have previously written or spoken, and this is clearly the case with 2 Timothy. Priscilla and Aquila clearly held a significant place in the unfolding story of the Gospel in the first century as they appeared in four books and the very last paragraph of Paul's final letter; they were apparently very dear to his heart.

How does the context inform the meaning of her story?

At that point in time, the Gospel of our Lord Jesus Christ was advancing throughout the known world, and specifically, the western world, and Priscilla and Aquila definitely played an important role in its advancement. No stranger to persecution or displacement, their adventures impacted major cities of influence and even nations.

As you examine their lives through the observation window, you will be delighted to learn about the people they knew and the places and times in which they lived. They left behind a trail of joyful celebration as many people under their faithful teaching found new life in Christ. We learn of their Jewish roots, Italian heritage, and industrious lifestyle through the narrative account found in Acts 18. We gain insight into their spiritual entrepreneurship through Paul's letters, as they both started and "grew" house churches, risking their very lives for the sake of the Gospel. Luke stated his purpose for writing the Gospel of Luke and the book of Acts clearly in:

- Luke 1:3-4 (NASB): **"Having investigated everything carefully from the beginning . . . so that you may know the exact truth about the things you have been taught."**

- Acts 1:1 (NASB): **"The first account I composed, Theophilus, about all that Jesus began to do and teach...."** indicates that it is the continuation of that same story of the Good News.

- Acts 1:8 (NASB): The Good News now reaching out through the people who place their faith in Jesus Christ to the **"remotest part of the earth"**

Couched within these pages, we find Priscilla, a strong woman of faith who is articulate, thoughtful, and evidently quite knowledgeable in her chosen profession, of current affairs of the Greco-Roman world, and most importantly, in the Word of God. Her strength enables her to work cooperatively, rather than combatively, with her husband Aquila.

Ecclesiastes 4:9-10 (NASB) states, **"Two are better than one because they have a good return for their labor. For if either of them falls, the one will lift up his companion. But woe to the one who falls when there is not another to lift him up."**

How do we know this about Aquila and Priscilla? Well, the text gives us several clues as well as definitive information. Of the six times they are mentioned in the Bible, they always appear together, and Priscilla's name appears first four times. This was highly unusual in Greco-Roman society and at this time in history. Together they found the biblical model of mutual submission to be a place of sweet surrender and successful service. Could it be that the chivalrous statement, "ladies first!" had its origins in the story of Priscilla and Aquila? As you study their story inductively, I am convinced that the Holy Spirit will give you fresh insights into relationship matters, and just why relationships matter so very much!

Herbert Lockyer in *All the Women of the Bible* says this:

> Priscilla's heart beat as one with her husband, Aquila. This unified couple was one in the Lord, one in vocation as tentmakers, one in their friendship with Paul, one in their profound knowledge of Scripture, and one in their service for the Church. They harmoniously labored together in the Lord's service, and they walked as one, for they had mutually agreed to put Christ first.[20]

Let's prepare our hearts to study as we succinctly pray the words of Psalm 119:18 (NASB): **"Open my eyes, that I may behold wonderful things from Your law."**

And…let's remember to pray! I don't want you to miss one single morsel of truth that God has for you as you study the life of Priscilla in God's Word. God is the Author of relationships, and when we pause to pray, stop, and listen well, I am convinced that we can hear His voice speaking softly, yet clearly, to our hearts. **"Your ears will hear a word behind you, "This is the way, walk in it," whenever you turn to the right or to the left"** (Isa. 30:21 NASB). As we ask, seek, and knock, He answers, yet His answers often come in gentle whispers that require an attentive heart, such as this encounter between Elijah the prophet, and the LORD found in 1 Kings 19:11-12 (NIV):

> **The LORD said, "Go out and stand on the mountain in the presence of the LORD, for the LORD is about to pass by." Then a great and powerful wind tore the**

---

[20] Herbert Lockyer, *All the Women of the Bible* (Grand Rapids: Zondervan, n.d.), 121-125.

mountains apart and shattered the rocks before the LORD, but the LORD was not in the wind. After the wind, there was an earthquake, but the LORD was not in the earthquake. After the earthquake came a fire, but the LORD was not in the fire. *And after the fire came a gentle whisper.*

Take time to pray. As you pray, take time to listen. Be still and know that He is God. God greatly desires to know you, love you, and reveal marvelous things to your heart about your relationship with Him and with others. I am convinced of this, and I am convinced that as we listen, *really listen*, God will speak!

The **Observation** window of inductive Bible study answers the question: **"What does the passage say?"**

Read the story of Priscilla at least two times. Again, I recommend reading two different translations of the Bible—one that is a word-for-word translation, like the English Standard Version, and one that is thought-for-thought, such as the New International Version. List the chapter and verse where you see the following facts.

It is helpful to read the section of Scripture before and after her story to provide more insight into the context. Avoid consulting study notes in your Bible or reference material until you have completed the observation window. This allows you to have an unfiltered perspective on what God's Word has to say, rather than an opinion of what someone else thinks God's Word has to say.

Who?

1. Make a list of each time Priscilla is mentioned in the story, by name or even by pronoun.

_____

_____

_____

_____

_____

_____

_____

_____

_____

_____

2. Make another list of all the people included in her story and how they interacted with one another.

_____

_____

_____

_____

_____

_____

_____

_____

3. Be sure to include a list of all references to God the Father, Jesus Christ, and the Holy Spirit. In addition, take special note of repeated words and phrases. There is a reason why things are listed more than once. Notice how others have forsaken God. What do their actions reveal? Who or what are they worshipping? What does God have to say about the way His people have forsaken Him?

I find this to be a good time to list words or phrases that I would like to research further, but I save that interesting research for later. For now, just list the facts. Once your list is complete, you're ready to ask the next questions.

_____

_____

_____

_____

_____

_____

Where?

1. Where did Priscilla live? Worship? Work? Travel?

_____

_____

_____

_____

_____

2. List all **places** in the story, as well as "where" words like inside, under, and behind that indicate location.

_____

_____

_____

_____

_____

When?

1. When did Priscilla live?

_____

_____

_____

_____

_____

2. List all other **time-related words** like "before" or "after," as well as when this takes place in the Bible according to the immediate context.

_____

_____

_____

_____

3. Notice the divine appointments that can only be explained by God Himself.

_____

_____

_____

_____

What?

1. What other important facts do we learn about Priscilla?

_____

_____

_____

_____

_____

2. What did Priscilla do, say, or contribute?

_____

_____

_____

_____

3. What problem did Priscilla create or resolve?

_____

_____

_____

_____

_____

_____

4. What is the single most significant contribution of her life? Her *essential?*

_____

_____

_____

_____

The observation phase prepares us for accurate interpretation as we ask, **"What do these facts mean to me?"** For example, ask yourself, **"What do I see as the reason God includes her story in His Word, the Bible?"** and **"What can I learn from her story to apply to my own life?"**

By now, I hope you have a fresh perspective on what the Holy Spirit is saying to you and how this story, and the truths within it, will impact your life. If you complete the observation of her story, and still have unanswered questions, then consult resources such as the notes in your study Bible, dictionaries, and commentaries, etc.

Interpretation

> **Interpretation** asks and answers the question: **"What does the story mean?"** Now that we have accurately observed the facts, we can properly interpret and discern the timeless truths that we learn from this biblical account.
>
> In this step, we will list at least two timeless truths from this story (there are usually more than two). The way that we determine if a truth is timeless is by asking: **"Is this true for all people, in all places, and at all times?"**

The following principles and practices of biblical interpretation help us to do just that.

1. **Pray** for wisdom, remembering that the primary purpose of Bible study is to change our lives, not simply to increase our knowledge.
2. **Establish the Bible as *the* authority.** It is the authoritative source of truth, given to us by God Himself (Heb. 4:12; 2 Tim. 3:16-17; Isa. 40:8).
3. **Recognize that the Bible interprets itself**; in other words, Scripture best explains Scripture. Pay attention to the context, cross-references, and repeated words and phrases, along with the type of literature.
4. **Interpret personal experience in the light of Scripture** and *not* Scripture in the light of personal experience. (Syncretism can result from seeing our cultural norms as if they are from God, rather than developing our cultural norms based on God's Word of truth.)
5. **Interpreting a text without context leads to pretext.** Biblical examples are authoritative only when supported by a command. Don't make a command from something that is intended as an illustration, such as Matthew 5:30: **"cut off your right hand."**

Here's <u>an example</u> of a timeless truth we learn from Priscilla's story:

Complete, don't compete. Mutually submissive relationships reveal the life and love of Christ.

The headless statue in this photo symbolizes the tyranny of leadership in the Roman era. Heads would roll, literally, each time a new leader came on the scene, replacing the statue with their own likeness. Rather than serving one another in love, they murdered one another and consequently lost the insight and wisdom of previous leaders. Time after time, Roman leaders exalted themselves on the shoulders of the past, and as a direct result, their reign ended in ruins. Perhaps we  can learn a lesson from this headless statue about how the Lord would have us lead those in our families, churches, and communities. Let us lead others following the example of our leader, the Lord Jesus who humbled Himself to death, even the death on a cross.[21] Paul encouraged the Macedonian church in Philippi along this path, saying,

> **Make my joy complete by being of the same mind, maintaining the same love, united in spirit, intent on one purpose. Do nothing from selfishness or empty conceit, but with humility of mind regard one another as more important than yourselves.** Phil. 2:2-3 NASB

As we, too, remember that we have this treasure in earthen vessels and that the surpassing greatness of the power may be of God and not from ourselves,[22] we are less likely to walk around this world like monsters, lopping off the heads of our opponents to our own demise.

If the early Christians in Macedonia and Achaia needed this lesson, surely those of us living in this age of "me, myself, and I" must learn it, apply it, and daily make its application our ambition so that we may decrease and He may increase (John 3:30 NASB). If so, then His joy will be made full—and so will ours!

Using these principles of interpretation, identify at least two timeless truths that are true for all people, in all places, at all times. Then, list the Bible verses where these truths are found in her story.

---

[21] Phil. 2:1-8.
[22] 2 Cor. 4:7ff.

Timeless Truth #1:
Verse(s):

Timeless Truth #2:
Verse(s):

If you have made it this far in your *Essentials* Bible study, congratulations! Most people do not try, nor do they complete, the hard work of **interpretation**. You have not only tried, but you also have successfully completed this step, and you are just about to reap the wonderful rewards of your diligent study as you discover how this unique story applies to you.

Application answers the question: **"What does this truth mean for me?"** and **"How do I live in response?"** It is time to apply God's timeless truths to our own lives and to experience the great fulfillment this brings as we move forward into spiritual maturity. This application window helps us to remember what we learn far more than if we only hear or read these truths. It empowers us to both know and do what the Bible says!

And remember, it is a message to obey, not just to listen to. If you do not obey, you are only fooling yourself. For if you just listen and do not obey, it is like looking at your face in a mirror but doing nothing to improve your appearance. You see yourself, walk away, and forget what you look like. But if you keep looking steadily into God's perfect law—and if you do what it says and don't forget what you heard, then God will bless you for doing it. James 1:22-25 NLT

If you are studying this as an individual, read over all the timeless truths you have uncovered. **If you are working with others,** gather in small groups, and read all the timeless truths you have discovered together out loud.

Determine which timeless truth is most relevant for you and other women in your target group. Read and respond to the following questions individually, or ask someone in the group to record your answers. You may only apply one or two of these questions as you develop an application to share, but it's good to review all of them as you prepare. And, there are seven of them so that we can ponder a different one each day of the week.

Ask, "Is there a/an _____?"

1. principle to apply
2. command to obey
3. attitude to change
4. sin to renounce
5. truth to believe
6. example to follow
7. specific action to take

This Bible study method helps you to *remember* and *apply* God's truth to your life—and to multiply that truth into the lives of other women.

If you are studying this Bible study as an individual, prepare a creative way to present your timeless truth through poetry, story, or drama, or reframe it as a current event news article.

If you are studying this as a small group, develop one of the following oral arts to express what you have learned. Create a meaningful:

- song
- dance
- artwork
- skit of a modern life drama from your community and nation
- poetry recitation
- story—yes, tell a story, maybe even *your* story!

When they didn't recognize Him at first after the resurrection, Jesus brought the disciples on the road to Emmaus into the biblical story, interpreting Scriptures for them in such a way that all of it started to make sense. Masterfully, He helped them to locate their own story in the context of the larger narrative of God's redemptive purposes in the world.[23]

Timeless truth to be presented:

_____

Method selected for presentation (song, dance, story, etc.):

_____

If you are studying with other women, each small group will present their application activity before they disclose which timeless truth they have chosen. Ask others what timeless truth they see through the application window.

---

[23] Ruth Haley Barton, *Life Together in Christ, Experiencing Transformation in Community* (Downers Grove, IL. InterVarsity Press, 2014).

My life is forever changed for the better because of the story of Priscilla and the timeless truths it teaches. All of us want to know that God's amazing and unchanging love extends all the way into our lives—I certainly do! As a woman, I must admit that I find great encouragement by seeing the key role given to women throughout His Word, but most especially in the New Testament. Truly, we women are joint-heirs with our brothers in Christ, as we equally share the privileges and responsibilities of living as His faithful followers. For "such a time as this" (as you will see later in Esther's story), Priscilla, you, and I are called to serve with humility and honor. This, my friend, is the express purpose of *Essentials* and is my prayer for you! May your life be forever changed and profoundly impacted, and may your potential be fully realized as a direct result of studying the lives of women, who, just like us, are evidence of His glory among all nations!

5 Reflection

Reflection is our final step, and yet it opens the window of our soul to receive the refreshing wind of the Holy Spirit. Engage in an activity that is refreshing for your soul: prayer, praise, journaling, lamenting, confession, silence, solitude, art, and/or nature appreciation. I like to call these soul food.

These are just a few examples, and others can be discovered and developed by studying Richard Foster's *Celebration of the Disciplines*, or my personal favorite, *The Spirit of the Disciplines* by Dallas Willard.

Jesus uses the analogy of sharing a meal with us in Revelation 3:20 (NLT): **"Look I stand at the door and knock. If you hear my voice and open the door, I will come in, and we will share a meal together as friends."**

Reflect on the beautiful gift of relationship through sharing a meal in community with a safe and affirming group of like-minded believers. Discuss the realities of relationships and learn from one another how you can become a more supportive friend, disciple, and partner in the Gospel—and how you can extend the greatest relationship of all, to those who don't yet know Christ as their Savior! If you are married, encourage other couples who share your aspiration to invite Christ into each meal and every aspect of marriage as you engage in meaningful dialogue. If you are single, don't limit your conversation about relationships to women only. Invite brothers in the faith to join you for the feast of healthy, holy, life-giving relationships, including, of course, some good food!

Consider these one-anothers as conversation starters (the Bible has more than 50 one-anothers):

- 1 Peter 5:14—"Greet one another."

- 1 Thessalonians 5:11—"Encourage one another."

- Galatians 5:13—"Serve one another in love."

Complete your time together with a prayer for one another!

5
BEAUTY THAT LASTS

I N THEIR FAMOUS song "Something," John, Paul, George, and Ringo—in perfect harmony—swoon over the one who has captured their heart and their attention simply with her moves, smile, and style. While her name is never given and her outward appearance is never described, she is forever etched on their collective hearts—and as a result—on the hearts of millions of fans.

As The Beatles rose to unrivaled stardom, the iconic lyrics of their classic 1969 song, "Something," were etched on the soul of every teenage girl. I well remember sitting in front of our black-and-white TV with wide-eyed wonder as thousands of teenage girls screamed at the mere sight of a Beatles performance. **Oh. My. Goodness.**

What Is Beauty?

Decades later, these hauntingly beautiful lyrics and melodies still evoke a mood, reflecting on a woman's beauty, and pull at the heart strings of every woman, or girl, who hears them. Why? Because woven into our psyche is the desire to have this same force of intrigue and unequaled attraction. We want to be beautiful. We equate outer beauty with the ability to achieve perfect relational results. For some people, beauty is even seen as a way to create a following, such as the **Influencer Movement** popular among many young women today. Still other women may find their careers advancing simply because of their outer beauty.

"Beauty is only skin deep," some may say, but millions of dollars are spent every year in an attempt to satisfy an unquenchable desire to increase our skin-deep beauty. Is this wrong? Not necessarily, but it may not yield quite the results we want. It may simply end with unfulfilled longings and empty pockets.

All the while, the Bible offers a stunning alternative. The beauty of a gentle and quiet spirit is of great worth in the eyes of God and offers a source of strength to all who know such a woman. The woman of worth described with detail in Proverbs 31:10-31 has beauty that is profoundly attractive, not from her external beauty, but rather it is her character qualities of diligence, compassion, faithfulness, and virtue that lend to her charm. Her "internal" wardrobe of strength and dignity radiates from her smile and twinkling eyes, which are both joyful in the present and confident of the future.

This type of beauty—beauty that lasts—is an *essential*. We are about to enter a story of one very beautiful young woman named Esther who discovered for herself that outer beauty does have some value, but beauty from within results in accolades that are literally out of this world.

> **There are many virtuous and capable women in the world,**
> **but you surpass them all! Charm is deceptive, and beauty does not last;**
> **but a woman who fears the LORD will be greatly praised.**
> **Reward her for all she has done.**
> **Let her deeds publicly declare her praise.** Prov. 31:29-31 NLT

Esther was known for her outer beauty. She joins the ranks of other beautiful women in the Bible such as Eve, Sarah, Rebekah, and Rachel. Rachel is also described as beautiful in both form and feature. Esther's beauty won her a place in the heart of King Xerxes. Even before she was presented to the king, she became the favorite of his chief servant Hegai, who oversaw the preparation of all the beautiful young virgins competing for the Queen's position. From this first introduction to Esther's beauty, we see the impeccable creative genius of our God as He weaves together her story. Yes, her outer beauty won her a place in the heart of the king, but it was her inner beauty and strength of character that enabled her to keep this position at a very critical time in Jewish history. We find that same strength of character leading her to the highest place of authority over the entire Persian kingdom that spanned from India to Ethiopia.

I don't want to give away all the intriguing morsels of truth that I learned from Esther, but I do want to whet your appetite and set the stage for active listening and learning. As you read the story of Esther once or twice from different versions of the Bible, here are some thought-provoking questions.

Esther is described as both beautiful and lovely, or "beautiful in form and feature," depending on the version of the Bible we read. Who helped Esther develop external beauty that won her great favor?

Is there something of an eternal nature to Esther's beauty?

If so, when and how do you see both her external and eternal beauty displayed?

Who did Esther rely upon and trust? How do we know?

What circumstances brought her eternal beauty to light?

What a promise we have in Esther's story! **Now, it's your turn! Grab your Bible and notepad with pen—or computer screen with touchpad or mouse—and get ready.** God will warm your heart with His love and enlighten your mind with His Truth. You will be transformed as you sit at His feet with a renewed sense of wonder!

Our first step in this Essentials narrative inductive Bible study is preparation. If you are teaching an *Essentials* Bible study group, or if you are simply studying on your own, here are three simple but vital steps to help you prepare well. Preparation is most definitely an essential. When we prepare a scrumptious recipe, we gather our ingredients, consider the temperature, and then proceed. In much the same way, we prepare for Bible study as we **read, research, and always remember to pray.**

READ her story in an essentially literal Bible translation (word-for-word) such as the English Standard Version and a dynamic equivalent version (thought-for-thought) such as the New Living Translation. Whenever possible, read out loud and more than once.

RESEARCH the background of the story to determine context and the type of literature, and to understand the writer's aim for the original audience. To get you started, I have shared some of my own notes with you below.

REMEMBER TO PRAY—God has something special to say to you through His Word. While the timeless truths in each story are for everyone, He understands you and your needs, and He wants to meet you right where you are. As you pray, you open your heart to receive His personal and practical Word of exhortation and hope.

Esther's story is found in the book of Esther, one of two books in the Bible named after women. Read the story of **Esther** more than once, and read it out loud. My preparation research revealed fascinating facts that inform our understanding of this *Essentials* study of Beauty through Esther's narrative.

Where is her story found, and who wrote it?

Esther is in the Old Testament. It is a book of history during the exile (diaspora/dispersion) of the Jews in 483-473 BC. Chronologically, Esther lived in the time period following the fall of both Israel and Judah, and just before the Silent Years between the two testaments, Old and New.

How does the context inform the meaning of this story?

Esther is one of the most intriguing books in the Bible. Keep reading to learn why.

God's power and purposes are evident at every turn, yet His relationship with His people had to be developed through the eyes of the people in Persia in this instance, rather than through those of the Israelites. God was about to reveal Himself to the people of Persia as He promised long before to Abraham and Sarah in Genesis 12:3 (NASB), **"…in you all the families of the earth shall be blessed."** The book of Esther demonstrates the way in which God works in a different culture, making the intrigue even more captivating. **Watch for it!** A Jewish woman was given full authority in the Persian culture. This is a total reversal of the way her predecessor, Vashti, was treated. Destiny was reversed, God was exalted, and women were honored.

The book is anonymous, but Jewish tradition maintains that Mordecai wrote it. One might wonder if Esther wrote this book as well based on Esther 9:29 (NASB): **"Then Queen Esther, daughter of Abihail, with Mordecai the Jew, wrote with full authority to confirm this second letter about Purim."** Mordecai received the privilege of writing with full authority along with Esther (Esther 8:8). Their words were written down by the scribes and published (Esther 8:13) for all the people in the Persian kingdom. Although some people have doubted the appropriateness of the book's presence in the Bible because of the lack of any direct mention of God, the book shows considerable evidence of the active involvement of God in Esther's life and the life of her people, the Jews. When we need Him the most, even if He seems the most absent, God just might be working in ways that exceed our imagination—more than we can ask, think, or imagine for all generations (Eph. 3:20-21).

REMEMBER TO PRAY:

We need to pray as we begin, as we study and research, and as we prepare to teach. Why do we make prayer such a significant part of Bible study? What's the big deal about prayer, you may ask? Remember, this is God's Word, and we need His input every step of the way. As we pray, God will bring to light just what He wants us to see. He will connect the dots within His Word and to cultural norms and individual lives in a way that is highly relevant and deeply personal all at once. He is the God of all wisdom, knowledge, and understanding.

Now you're ready to open and meet Esther through the window of observation.

The **Observation** window of inductive Bible study answers the question: **"What does the passage say?"**

Read the story of Esther at least two times. Again, I recommend reading two different translations of the Bible—one that is a word-for-word translation, like the English Standard Version, and one that is thought-for-thought, such as the New International Version. List the chapter and verse where you see the following facts.

It is helpful to read the section of Scripture before and after her story to provide more insight into the context. Avoid consulting study notes in your Bible or reference material until you have completed the observation window. This allows you to have an unfiltered perspective on what God's Word has to say, rather than an opinion of what someone else thinks God's Word has to say.

Esther's story is longer than any of our other "Essentials," so be sure to give yourself enough time to read and record your answers to the observation questions that follow. If you are studying with a group, study Esther in two sections: Chapters 1 through 5 and then Chapters 6 through 10. That way you won't miss a single nugget of truth or essence of beauty that God has lovingly placed within the pages of her story!

Who?

1. Make a list of each time Esther is mentioned in the story, by name or even by pronoun.

_____

_____

_____

_____

_____

_____

_____

2. Make another list of all the people included in her story and how they interacted with one another.

   For example: How did Esther interact with other people listed in the story, especially the king? What did she call him and know about him?

   _____

   _____

   _____

   _____

   _____

   _____

   _____

   _____

3. Be sure to include a list of all references to God the Father, Jesus Christ, and the Holy Spirit. And, in the book of Esther, in addition, take special note of repeated words and phrases. There is a reason why things are listed more than once. Notice how others have forsaken God. What do their actions reveal? Who or what are they worshipping? What does God have to say about the way His people have forsaken Him?

   I find this to be a good time to list words or phrases that I would like to research further, but I save that interesting research for later. For now, just list the facts. Once your list is complete, you're ready to ask the next questions.

   _____

   _____

   _____

   _____

   _____

   _____

Interestingly, Esther's name is mentioned 47 times, but the Jews are mentioned 48 times. As you read, note how the Jews are included, disgraced, and protected by God and His divine authority released through Esther. These observations will help you interpret the rich meaning of this story as timeless truths. And it will release the power of the Holy Spirit to apply these same truths into your own life with the authority of God's Word.

_____

_____

_____

_____

_____

_____

Where?

1. Where did Esther live? Worship? Work? Travel?

_____

_____

_____

_____

_____

2. List all **places** in the story, as well as "where" words like inside, under, and behind that indicate location.

_____

_____

_____

_____

_____

When?

1. When did Esther live?

_____

_____

_____

_____

_____

2. List all other **time-related words** like "before" or "after," as well as when this takes place in the Bible according to the immediate context.

_____

_____

_____

_____

3. Notice the divine appointments that can only be explained by God Himself.

_____

_____

_____

_____

_____

_____

_____

What?

1. What other important facts do we learn about Esther?

_____

_____

_____

_____

_____

_____

_____

2. What did Esther do, say, or contribute?

_____

_____

_____

_____

_____

_____

_____

3. What problem did Esther create or resolve?

_____

_____

_____

_____

_____

4. What is the single most significant contribution of her life? Her *essential?*

_____

_____

_____

I just hate it when someone misinterprets and then misappropriates something said about me. How about you? The very same thing is true of God. He makes that clear in this verse and others like it: **"Do your best to present yourself to God as one approved, a worker who has no need to be ashamed, rightly handling the word of truth"** (2 Tim. 2:15 ESV).

So, as you have taken the time to observe the facts about Esther with great detail, you can have confidence that God approves. The Bible is clear that the Old Testament stories are not just fables, but rather they are real-life examples to equip, warn, and prepare us well: **"Now these things happened to them as an example *and* warning [to us]; they were written for our instruction [to admonish and equip us], upon whom the ends of the ages have come"** (1 Cor. 10:11 AMP).

We have noted that the book of Esther is unique, as God is not named; rather, He is identified through His people, the Jews. I want you to remember the purpose behind this. Why did God identify Himself in and through the Jews? Is God only the God of the Jews? Or, is He including all peoples and nations in His Promise?

He had a distinct purpose for the Jews, as noted in Genesis 12:3 (ESV), **"in you all the families of the earth shall be blessed."** The fact that God wanted the Jews to point the nations to God is mentioned multiple times throughout the Old Testament. Some wonderful examples are Exodus 19:4-6 and Deuteronomy 7:6.

Then, in the New Testament, we see Jesus, the Messiah, fulfill this purpose in the Gospels. And, just before He returns to Heaven, He says, **"You will be My witnesses...even to the ends of the earth"** (Acts 1:8 AMP).

I hope you are eager to move forward, well-equipped to fearlessly face the future and share this Good News with others, displaying His beauty from the inside out. Remember, His promise is inclusive, not exclusive:

> **The Spirit and the Bride say, "Come." And let the one who hears say, "Come." And let the one who is thirsty come; let the one who desires take the water of life without price.**
> Rev. 22:17 ESV

3 Interpretation

> **Interpretation** asks and answers the question: **"What does the story mean?"** Now that we have accurately observed the facts, we can properly interpret and discern the timeless truths that we learn from this biblical account.
>
> In this step, we will list at least two timeless truths from this story (there are usually more than two). The way that we determine if a truth is timeless is by asking: **"Is this true for all people, in all places, and at all times?"**

The following principles and practices of biblical interpretation help us to do just that.

1. **Pray** for wisdom, remembering that the primary purpose of Bible study is to change our lives, not simply to increase our knowledge.
2. **Establish the Bible as *the* authority.** It is the authoritative source of truth, given to us by God Himself (Heb. 4:12; 2 Tim. 3:16-17; Isa. 40:8).
3. **Recognize that the Bible interprets itself**; in other words, Scripture best explains Scripture. Pay attention to the context, cross-references, and repeated words and phrases, along with the type of literature.
4. **Interpret personal experience in the light of Scripture** and *not* Scripture in the light of personal experience. (Syncretism can result from seeing our cultural norms as if they are from God, rather than developing our cultural norms based on God's Word of truth.)
5. **Interpreting a text without context leads to pretext.** Biblical examples are authoritative only when supported by a command. Don't make a command from something that is intended as an illustration, such as Matthew 5:30: **"cut off your right hand."**

Here's an example of a timeless truth we learn from Esther's story:

Beauty can be a platform for a godly example, regardless of your age. **"Let no one look down on your youthfulness, but rather in speech, conduct, love, faith, and purity, show yourself an example of those who believe"** (1 Tim. 4:12 NASB).

Using these principles of interpretation, identify at least two timeless truths that are true for all people, in all places, at all times. Then, list the Bible verses where these truths are found in Esther's story.

Timeless Truth #1:
Verse(s):

Timeless Truth #2:
Verse(s):

Application

Application answers the question: **"What does this truth mean for me?"** and **"How do I live in response?"** It is time to apply God's timeless truths to our own lives and to experience the great fulfillment this brings as we move forward into spiritual maturity. This application window helps us to remember what we learn far more than if we only hear or read these truths. It empowers us to both know and do what the Bible says!

And remember, it is a message to obey, not just to listen to. If you do not obey, you are only fooling yourself. For if you just listen and do not obey, it is like looking at your face in a mirror but doing nothing to improve your appearance. You see yourself, walk away, and forget what you look like. But if you keep looking steadily into God's perfect law—and if you do what it says and don't forget what you heard, then God will bless you for doing it. James 1:22-25 NLT

If you are studying this as an individual, read over all the timeless truths you have uncovered. **If you are working with others,** gather in small groups, and read all the timeless truths you have discovered together out loud.

Determine which timeless truth is most relevant for you and other women in your target group. Read and respond to the following questions individually, or ask someone in the group to record your answers. You may only apply one or two of these questions as you develop an application to share, but it's good to review all of them as you prepare.

Ask, "Is there a/an _____?"

1. principle to apply
2. command to obey
3. attitude to change
4. sin to renounce
5. truth to believe
6. example to follow
7. specific action to take

This Bible study method helps you to *remember* and *apply* God's truth to your life—and to multiply that truth into the lives of other women.

If you are studying this Bible study as an individual, prepare a creative way to present your timeless truth through poetry, story, or drama, or reframe it as a current event news article.

If you are studying this as a small group, develop one of the following oral arts to express what you have learned. Create a meaningful:

- song
- dance
- artwork
- skit of a modern life drama from your community and nation
- poetry recitation
- story—yes, tell a story, maybe even *your* story!

Timeless truth to be presented:

_____

Method selected for presentation (song, dance, story, etc.):

_____

If you are studying with other women, each small group will present their application activity before they disclose which timeless truth they have chosen. Ask others what timeless truth they see through the application window.

Reflection is our final step, and yet it opens the window of our soul to receive the refreshing wind of the Holy Spirit. Engage in an activity that is refreshing for your soul: prayer, praise, journaling, lamenting, confession, silence, solitude, art, and/or nature appreciation. I like to call these soul food.

These are just a few examples, and others can be discovered and developed by studying Richard Foster's *Celebration of the Disciplines*, or my personal favorite, *The Spirit of the Disciplines* by Dallas Willard.

Just how do we include reflection or spiritual renewal in our Bible study? After discovering a timeless truth, take some time to reflect on this truth with the help of the Holy Spirit. Include a spiritual practice such as solitude or silence, or determine to pray each day for one month as you wait to see what God will do. Celebration is an equally important discipline and one that was required by God's chosen people as they entered the Promised Land. Celebration and worship can take place in various places, spaces, and forms. One of the hidden gems in the book of Esther is the fact that God is not readily apparent at first glance. **But is He absent? Or is He hidden in plain sight?**

Think about this. Ponder the reality of God in Esther's story and then develop a creative way to worship Him in an artform that you enjoy. Even if you don't consider yourself a great artist, this activity will enhance your worship and deepen your praise!

Your time of reflection might include a day, or a half-day, solitude retreat. Take your Bible, journal, and a pen, and sit alone in nature or in a special corner of your home, as you wait and listen for His voice.

Reflection strengthens us from within. It enables us to know and treasure our Savior as our highest Essential, too. I am convinced that as we do, we will understand just how our story is truly part of God's global redemption Story, by which we can join our story with the stories of other people so that they can love Him too!

Contemplating the Story of Esther

As I read and studied this story inductively, I found myself praising God for the way He created women and for the unique differences between men and women. I rejoice in all that we can learn from one another. The way men and women lead together in the Bible fascinates and delights me. Esther and Mordecai are an intriguing example of this dual, shared leadership. Their strengths, rather than their gender differences, dictate the scope and extent of their authority from India to Ethiopia, which was essentially the entire known and civilized world at that time (and interestingly, most of the 10/40 window!).

Since I have personally traveled to 44 nations (so far!), and many of them within this region, I marvel at the way in which God opened up His world through the obedience and the beauty of a woman, who was accompanied and mentored by a man who clearly believed in her potential.

My personal contemplative worship activity will include a visit to the cemetery where my Dad is buried. I well remember his encouragement, sense of humor, and insistence on taking me to the airport every single time I traveled both internationally and domestically for nearly 20 years.

I will bring flowers and spend time thanking our Creator God for creating him as a man who loved me as his daughter and always cheered me on to new and higher heights as a woman leader.

Remembering has great power. It is an essential part of the story of Esther. Purim, a Jewish feast of remembrance, was instituted by Esther and Mordecai because of the victory over evil. It is celebrated to this very day by Jews around the world as they read the book of Esther, together and out loud. Let's reread this portion to remember what we have learned:

> **So these days were to be remembered and celebrated throughout every generation, every family, every province and every city; and these days of Purim were not to fail from among the Jews, or their memory fade from their descendants.**

> **Then Queen Esther, daughter of Abihail, with Mordecai the Jew, wrote with full authority to confirm this second letter about Purim. He sent letters to all the Jews, to the 127 provinces of the kingdom of Ahasuerus, *namely,* words of peace and truth, to establish these days of Purim at their appointed times, just as Mordecai the Jew and Queen Esther had established for them, and just as they had established for themselves and for their descendants with instructions for their times of fasting and their lamentations. The command of Esther established these customs for Purim, and it was written in the book.** Esther 9:28-32 NASB

Perhaps you do not have fond memories of the men in your life, both past and present. In that case, as you contemplate the story of Esther, remember the Lord and His wonderful works. Let Him wash over the memories of your past and lead you into a new future of hope and strength in His presence:

> **Seek the LORD and His strength; Seek His face continually.**
> **Remember His wonders which He has done,**
> **His marvels and the judgments uttered by His mouth.**
> Ps. 105:4-5 NASB

6
EDUCATION THAT HAS AN IMPACT

WOMEN HAVE A passion for education. From the first pages of the Bible to its final chapters, we see the evidence and results of our quest for knowledge. Huldah the prophetess will be the focus of this chapter. Is Huldah unique? One of a kind? Through this study, we will see how women from the pages of the Bible, and throughout history, were eager to learn and grow in their understanding of God and this world. We'll also see how we can have an impact today, tomorrow, and throughout eternity.

Did you know that women are just as likely as men to receive college degrees? The influx in recent decades of college-educated women has driven their numbers to record levels. Current trends reveal that more college students are female, including women of color and those from many different ethnic backgrounds.[24] Women are

---

[24] U.S. Census Bureau, "College Degree Widens Gender Earnings Gap," The United States Census Bureau, May 29, 2019, https://www.census.gov/library/stories/2019/05/college-degree-widens-gender-earnings-gap.html.

eagerly pursuing higher education, and many are receiving advanced degrees. They are lifting the glass ceiling, so to speak, and in some places, they've broken it altogether.

In other parts of the world, disparity between education levels of men and women, even between boys and girls, still exists. Consider these facts researched and recorded by the United Nations: Rural women's deficits in education have long-term implications for family well-being and poverty reduction. Data from 68 countries indicates that a woman's education is a key factor in determining a child's survival.[25]

> Data from 68 countries indicates that a woman's education is a key factor in determining a child's survival.

In other words, when women are given the opportunity to receive an adequate education, their families, communities, and even their nations benefit. The next generation not only survives, but they also begin to thrive. This is a trend that is on the rise in the twenty-first century, and we can trace its origin and intention to the influence of our Savior, the Lord Jesus Christ.

However, this was not always the case. Hebrew, Greek, and Roman cultures forbade—or at the very least, hindered—the education of women and girls. And while neither Christ nor his apostles officially promoted a women's "movement," Christ's message of repentance and salvation had revolutionary effects on the lives of women. His life and teaching began to shape the culture in significant ways:

> While Christians were not the first to engage in formal teaching…they appear to have been first to teach both sexes in the same setting. Given that Christianity from its beginning accepted both men and women into its fold and required that both learn the rudiments of the Christian faith—in teaching both sexes, Christians took their cue from Jesus, who never had a problem teaching women along with men. Co-education appears to be a product of Jesus Christ's wholesome influence.[26]

Pandita Ramabai, Mary Mcleod Bethune, Anne Frank, Linda Matar, and Eunice Otieno are just a few examples of women who pursued an education and, as a result, made this world a better place for us all. God created us with a passion for learning and using what we learn to make a difference in the lives of others. As more women pursue professional degrees, they enter a wide array of careers, which include medicine, law, teaching, and engineering. They are becoming entrepreneurs who provide vital services

---

[25] "Facts & Figures," UN Women, accessed October 19, 2020, https://www.unwomen.org/en/news/in-focus/commission-on-the-status-of-women-2012/facts-and-figures.

[26] Alvin J. Schmidt, *How Christianity Changed the World: Formerly Titled Under the Influence* (Grand Rapids, MI: Zondervan, 2004).

and creative products to individuals, families, and communities through micro and macro businesses.

We no longer limit ourselves based on societal expectations. And, while formal education is an excellent option for women, it is not our *only* option. Non-formal education via internships and international partnerships is shaping the future of how women serve both God and other people.

Yes, the pages of history reveal our thirst for knowledge and our powerful, life-changing impact as women. So do the pages of the Bible. Ruth learned from Naomi, Esther from Mordecai, and Apollos from Priscilla and Aquila. God demonstrates through real-life examples within the pages of His Word that His desire is for both men and women, boys and girls, to be educated in all of His ways:

> **All your children shall be taught by the LORD, and great shall be the peace of your children.** Isa. 54:13 ESV

Jesus quotes the Isaiah 54:13 passage directly in John 6:45 when speaking with the Jewish leaders of His time. Not only did He preach about including both girls and boys in the learning process, but He also demonstrated it multiple times. Mary of Bethany sat at the feet of Jesus to listen and learn. Jesus commended her for this, stating that she had chosen the "good part" that will not be taken from her (Luke 10:38-42). Clearly, women were part of His inner circle of support and discipleship (Luke 8:1-3).

From the classroom (formal), from the chair of the apprentice (non-formal), and from the heart of a mentor or a trusted friend (informal)—education is essential and comes to us in many different forms. God created us, both male and female, to learn and grow with shared dominion over all of His creation. While the Bible is not an academic textbook, it clearly reveals that this learning and studying of His creation is something God has declared to be good. When men and women learn and work together, complementing one another with their strengths and talents, God declares it is *very good* (Gen. 1:27-31).

How wonderful it is that Jesus invites us all, both men and women, to learn directly from Him:

> **Come to Me, all you who labor and are heavy-laden and overburdened, and I will cause you to rest—I will ease and relieve and refresh your souls. Take My yoke upon you, and learn of Me, for I am gentle (meek) and humble (lowly) in heart, and you will find rest—relief, ease and refreshment, and recreation and blessed quiet—for your souls.** Matt. 11:28-29 AMP

Women were the last at the cross, the first at the empty tomb, and the first to be sent to preach the Good News of the Gospel to the apostles. Christ's practice of educating and including women continued into the upper room as the disciples waited for the outpouring of the Holy Spirit: **"These all with one mind were continually devoting themselves to prayer, along with the women, and Mary the mother of Jesus, and with His brothers"** (Acts 1:14 NASB). From this point forward, we have all been sent to be His witnesses in our own Jerusalem, to Judea, and to the uttermost parts of the earth.

This invitation became the sole ambition of the Apostle Paul, who was considered a Hebrew scholar, highly educated by any standard. His chief educational pursuit was radically altered on the road to Damascus, as recorded in Acts 9. Paul's life took a radical turn from that moment on. Difficulties beyond description were his common lot. God shaped and molded him into a new man through the trials he experienced. He emerged from this plight with the passion of an apostle and the heart of a pastor. His unceasing prayer for the Christians at Colossae, and all who trust Christ as Savior, became, **"that you may be filled with the knowledge of His will in all spiritual wisdom and understanding"** (Col. 1:9 NASB). In another of Paul's letters, we find his prayer with these beautiful Life-giving words: **"He predestined us to adoption as sons through Jesus Christ to Himself, according to the kind intention of His will to the praise of the glory of His grace"** (Eph. 1:5 NASB).

Paul came to see that the ultimate education of head and heart is to learn and understand **"the kind intention of His will."** Let that phrase sink in. Meditate on it, repeat it out loud a time or two. If you are facing a crisis of your own, I want you to remember and reflect, and then rejoice in the kind intention of His will for you, and for all that pertains to you—every single aspect of your life, everything, and everyone.

I am thrilled there is more space in our modern culture for a woman's education and professional impact. Each of us has an essential role to play. Yet, if I'm really honest, I am even more passionate about the insight, decorum, and wisdom women can bring into any given situation when they understand and express the kind intention of God's will. I have observed situations where men were gridlocked in conversation, and a woman of dignity and courage spoke a word of wisdom, diffusing the tension and conflict. It is clear to me that women are essential in the boardroom, the hospital, the courtroom, as well as every room in the house.

Education, in its essence, provides an opportunity to demonstrate the kind intentionality of our God, whatever our field of expertise. Ladies, do not neglect the slightest prospect to further your education, knowing that it offers you a platform by which to display the One who is perfect in knowledge, understanding, and wisdom.

"For truly my words are not false, One who is perfect in knowledge is with you" (Job 36:4 NASB).

It is now my esteemed privilege to introduce you to an astute and knowledgeable woman named Huldah. Although her educational resume is not disclosed, she had earned the respect of her community for her knowledge of God's Word and the wisdom she had gained from it. She had hidden God's Word in her heart so that she would not sin against Him (Ps. 119:11). She was a vessel of honor, fit for the Master's service (2 Tim. 2:21), and her moment of high and holy service was just about to arrive.

Our first step in this Essentials narrative inductive Bible study is preparation. **If you are teaching an *Essentials* Bible study group, or if you are simply studying on your own, here are three simple but vital steps to help you prepare well.** Preparation is most definitely an essential. When we prepare a scrumptious recipe, we gather our ingredients, consider the temperature, and then proceed. In much the same way, we prepare for Bible study as we **read, research, and always remember to pray.**

READ her story in an essentially literal Bible translation (word-for-word) such as the English Standard Version and a dynamic equivalent version (thought-for-thought) such as the New Living Translation. Whenever possible, read out loud and more than once.

RESEARCH the background of the story to determine context and the type of literature, and to understand the writer's aim for the original audience. To get you started, I have shared some of my own notes with you below.

REMEMBER TO PRAY—God has something special to say to you through His Word. While the timeless truths in each story are for everyone, He understands you and your needs, and He wants to meet you right where you are. As you pray, you open your heart to receive His personal and practical Word of exhortation and hope.

Where is her story found, and who wrote it?

Huldah's story is found in the Old Testament books of 2 Kings 22:14-20 and 2 Chronicles 34:22-33 (full context: 2 Kings 22 through 23:30 and 2 Chronicles 34-35).

These two historical records validate the facts of her story with their full agreement. The authors of both Kings and Chronicles are uncertain. What is certain, however, is that God's Word provides a very careful and detailed account of the history of His people from approximately 1000 to 500 BC. God wants us to learn from the example of His people, the Jews, in their cycles of sin, desperation, and restoration—and, as it turns out, from the life of a woman named Huldah, who confidently interpreted the Word of God for the king of Judah.

How does the context inform the meaning of this story?

Let's take a few minutes to reflect on how significant her story is as we review what was happening in this period of history. The children of Israel, called to be God's chosen people, had largely chosen *against* Him. They not only turned their hearts against God time and time again, but they also demanded to be like the other nations around them that had their own kings. The prophet Samuel, Hannah's firstborn son, warned them against the tyranny and possible destruction that would result from having human rulers, but they were adamant; they wanted a king, and they would have a king. No one was going to stop them.

First, Saul, followed by David, and then his son, Solomon, ruled the nation of Israel, which at that point became known as the kingdom of Israel. The Israelites rebelled and fell into sin, easily led astray by false idol worship of the nations surrounding them, and soon were divided into two kingdoms—Israel to the north and Judah to the south. After many cycles of sin and restoration, the northern kingdom of Israel was conquered by the Assyrians. The kingdom of Judah remained in its native land, but not for very long. It soon followed the same treacherous cycle of sin, captivity, restoration, and repeated sin, and was eventually taken captive by the Babylonians.

The Bible designates the various kings of Israel and Judah as "good" or "evil." Evil kings reveled in self-serving practices that shunned God and hurt their people. Their actions mirrored the hideous practices of the nations around them. Good kings followed the ways of the Lord God with wholehearted devotion, sincere worship, and lives of love for the people they were called to serve. God sent prophets to help and often warn the kings of Israel and Judah. Among them, the prophets Jeremiah and Zephaniah were contemporaries of Huldah.

Across this storm-tossed sea of sinful humanity, we glimpse a tiny sailboat navigating the tumultuous waves. The sails of this boat glisten as they reflect the Sun of righteousness (see Luke 1:78). This tiny sailboat depicts the life of Huldah, the prophetess, divinely appointed and strategically positioned to reflect God's truth with grace. The wind of the Holy Spirit carried her along the repeated waves of her people's sinful cycle of despair and destruction. Finally, at just the right place, and in just the right time, she became the voice God used to redirect and strengthen His people through His Holy Word—a word fitly spoken to the king. Grab your Bible and notepad, and get ready. As you observe the details in Huldah's account, God will warm your heart with His love and enlighten your mind with wonder!

The **Observation** window of inductive Bible study answers the question: **"What does the passage say?"**

Read the story of Huldah at least two times. Again, I recommend reading two different translations of the Bible—one that is a word-for-word translation, like the English Standard Version, and one that is thought-for-thought, such as the New International Version. List the chapter and verse where you see the following facts.

It is helpful to read the section of Scripture before and after her story to provide more insight into the context. Avoid consulting study notes in your Bible or reference material until you have completed the observation window. This allows you to have an unfiltered perspective on what God's Word has to say, rather than an opinion of what someone else thinks God's Word has to say.

Who?

1. Make a list of each time Huldah is mentioned in the story, by name or even by pronoun.

2. Make another list of all the people included in her story and how they interacted with one another.

_____

_____

_____

_____

_____

_____

_____

_____

3. Be sure to include a list of all references to God the Father, Jesus Christ, and the Holy Spirit. In addition, take special note of repeated words and phrases. There is a reason why things are listed more than once. Notice how others have forsaken God. What do their actions reveal? Who or what are they worshipping? What does God have to say about the way His people have forsaken Him?

I find this to be a good time to list words or phrases that I would like to research further, but I save that interesting research for later. For now, just list the facts. Once your list is complete, you're ready to ask the next questions.

_____

_____

_____

_____

_____

_____

Where?

1. Where did Huldah live? Worship? Work? Travel?

_____

_____

_____

_____

_____

2. List all **places** in the story, as well as "where" words like inside, under, and behind that indicate location.

_____

_____

_____

_____

_____

When?

1. When did Huldah live?

_____

_____

_____

_____

_____

2. List all other **time-related words** like "before" or "after," as well as when this takes place in the Bible according to the immediate context.

_____

_____

_____

_____

3. Notice the divine appointments that can only be explained by God Himself.

_____

_____

_____

_____

_____

What?

1. What other important facts do we learn about Huldah?

_____

_____

_____

_____

2. What did Huldah do, say, or contribute?

_____

_____

_____

_____

3. What problem did Huldah create or resolve?

_____

_____

_____

_____

_____

_____

4. What is the single most significant contribution of her life? Her *essential*?

_____

_____

_____

The observation phase prepares us for accurate interpretation as we ask, **"What do these facts mean to me?"** For example, ask yourself, **"What do I see as the reason God includes her story in His Word, the Bible?"** and **"What can I learn from her story to apply to my own life?"**

By now, I hope you have a fresh perspective on what the Holy Spirit is saying to you and how this story, and the truths within it, will impact your life. If you complete the observation of her story, and still have unanswered questions, then consult resources such as the notes in your study Bible, dictionaries, and commentaries, etc.

Interpretation asks and answers the question: **"What does the story mean?"** Now that we have accurately observed the facts, we can properly interpret and discern the timeless truths that we learn from this biblical account.

In this step, we will list at least two timeless truths from this story (there are usually more than two). The way that we determine if a truth is timeless is by asking: **"Is this true for all people, in all places, and at all times?"**

The following principles and practices of biblical interpretation help us to do just that.

1. **Pray** for wisdom, remembering that the primary purpose of Bible study is to change our lives, not simply to increase our knowledge.
2. **Establish the Bible as *the* authority.** It is the authoritative source of truth, given to us by God Himself (Heb. 4:12; 2 Tim. 3:16-17; Isa. 40:8).
3. **Recognize that the Bible interprets itself**; in other words, Scripture best explains Scripture. Pay attention to the context, cross-references, and repeated words and phrases, along with the type of literature.
4. **Interpret personal experience in the light of Scripture** and *not* Scripture in the light of personal experience. (Syncretism can result from seeing our cultural norms as if they are from God, rather than developing our cultural norms based on God's Word of truth.)
5. **Interpreting a text without context leads to pretext.** Biblical examples are authoritative only when supported by a command. Don't make a command from something that is intended as an illustration, such as Matthew 5:30: **"cut off your right hand."**

Example: People often misuse the Bible to justify their sinful behavior by interpreting it out of context. An individual may say, "God wants me to be filled with joy and enjoy my love life (Song of Songs 2:4). He promises to give me the desires of my heart (Ps. 37:5). My wife or husband no longer fills me with joy. So, my heart's desire is for a new spouse. Consequently, it is perfectly fine for me to divorce them." This may seem extreme, but it happens more often than we care to acknowledge; it serves as an example of why it is vital to accurately interpret our experiences based on God's Word, not the other way around.

Using these principles of interpretation, identify at least two or more timeless truths that are true for all people, in all places, at all times. List the Bible verses where these truths are found in Huldah's story.

Interpretation is possibly one of the most challenging aspects of inductive Bible study, but it's also an absolutely essential one! What do we gain from simply storing up knowledge in our mind, if we don't take the time to accurately interpret it?

Timeless Truth #1:
Verse(s):

Timeless Truth #2:
Verse(s):

Application answers the question: **"What does this truth mean for me?"** and **"How do I live in response?"** It is time to apply God's timeless truths to our own lives and to experience the great fulfillment this brings as we move forward into spiritual maturity. This application window helps us to remember what we learn far more than if we only hear or read these truths. It empowers us to both know and do what the Bible says!

And remember, it is a message to obey, not just to listen to. If you do not obey, you are only fooling yourself. For if you just listen and do not obey, it is like looking at your face in a mirror but doing nothing to improve your appearance. You see yourself, walk away, and forget what you look like. But if you keep looking steadily into God's perfect law—and if you do what it says and don't forget what you heard, then God will bless you for doing it. James 1:22-25 NLT

If you are studying this as an individual, read over all the timeless truths you have uncovered. **If you are working with others,** gather in small groups, and read all the timeless truths you have discovered together out loud.

Determine which timeless truth is most relevant for you and other women in your target group. Read and respond to the following questions individually, or ask someone in the group to record your answers. You may only apply one or two of these questions as you develop an application to share, but it's good to review all of them as you prepare.

Ask, "Is there a/an _____?"

1. principle to apply
2. command to obey
3. attitude to change
4. sin to renounce
5. truth to believe
6. example to follow
7. specific action to take

This Bible study method helps you to *remember* and *apply* God's truth to your life—and to multiply that truth into the lives of other women.

If you are studying this Bible study as an individual, prepare a creative way to present your timeless truth through poetry, story, or drama, or reframe it as a current event news article.

If you are studying this as a small group, develop one of the following oral arts to express what you have learned. Create a meaningful:

- song
- dance
- artwork
- skit of a modern life drama from your community and nation
- poetry recitation
- story—yes, tell a story, maybe even *your* story!

Timeless truth to be presented:

_____

Method selected for presentation (song, dance, story, etc.):

_____

If you are studying with other women, each small group will present their application activity before they disclose which timeless truth they have chosen. Ask others what timeless truth they see through the application window.

Together, we can become a global community of women—trustworthy witnesses of the saving grace of Christ Jesus, fulfilling His Great Commission with Great Commandment love:

> **You have heard me teach things that have been confirmed by many reliable witnesses. Now teach these truths to other trustworthy people who will be able to pass them on to others.** 2 Tim. 2:2 NLT

Reflection

> **Reflection** is our final step, and yet it opens the window of our soul to receive the refreshing wind of the Holy Spirit. Engage in an activity that is refreshing for your soul: prayer, praise, journaling, lamenting, confession, silence, solitude, art, and/or nature appreciation. I like to call these soul food.
>
> These are just a few examples, and others can be discovered and developed by studying Richard Foster's *Celebration of the Disciplines*,[27] or my personal favorite, *The Spirit of the Disciplines*[28] by Dallas Willard.

I invite you to look out the window of reflection through Huldah's story. Imagine how she may have felt year after year, decade after decade, as she watched the ruinous cycle of sin among her people, and especially the leaders of her people.

What books did she read? What lessons did she learn at the feet of those she trusted in her own generation and from earlier generations? What was the essential lesson she felt compelled to pass on to the next generation?

Select the contemplative method that best enables you to complete your study of Huldah, and then make it a priority on your calendar. You might want to enjoy a more in-depth study of Huldah from several commentaries, Bible dictionaries, and other references.

Have you decided which reflection practice best suits you and this specific study of Huldah's story? Contemplative Bible reading, also called *Lectio Divina*, includes these steps:

- Reading/listening
- Meditating
- Praying
- Contemplating

---

[27] Richard J. Foster, *Celebration of Discipline: the Path to Spiritual Growth* (San Francisco: HarperOne, 2018).

[28] Dallas Willard, *The Spirit of the Disciplines: Understanding How God Changes Lives* (Grand Rapids, MI: Family Christian Press, 2001).

Education that has an impact begins with the mind but penetrates and transforms the heart. Jesus was an exemplary teacher whose words deeply spoke into people's lives. Often called the Sermon on the Mount, the Beatitudes are part of His longest discourse. Consider reading them daily through the lens of contemplative Bible reading as you meditate, pray, and reflect in writing.

The following is a Reflection opportunity for you.

I chose to focus my contemplative attention on **the Beatitudes** in the New Testament book of Matthew and to read the Beatitudes each day for five days, taking special note of the specific behaviors that He promotes and the promises that follow. I spent time reading, meditating, praying, and reflecting on the impact of each beatitude as I asked:

- How is the teaching found in the Beatitudes counterintuitive to our lives today?

- Which one seems most difficult for me?

- Which one do I most need to include in my personal relationship with God?

- Which one do I most need and desire to reflect in my life and relationships?

- Which one would I most appreciate seeing and hearing from a close friend or colleague?

Read the Beatitudes found in Matthew 5:2-12 (ESV):

> **And he opened his mouth and taught them, saying:**
> **Blessed are the poor in spirit, for theirs is the kingdom of heaven.**
> **Blessed are those who mourn, for they shall be comforted.**
> **Blessed are the meek, for they shall inherit the earth.**
> **Blessed are those who hunger and thirst for righteousness, for they shall be satisfied.**
> **Blessed are the merciful, for they shall receive mercy.**
> **Blessed are the pure in heart, for they shall see God.**
> **Blessed are the peacemakers, for they shall be called sons of God.**
> **Blessed are those who are persecuted for righteousness' sake, for theirs is the kingdom of heaven.**
> **Blessed are you when others revile you and persecute you and utter all kinds of evil against you falsely on my account.**
> **Rejoice and be glad, for your reward is great in heaven, for so they persecuted the prophets who were before you.**

Write a poem or essay that reflects the strength and wisdom you "see" in the life of Huldah as you read, meditate, pray, and contemplate the Beatitudes. Below are some thought-provoking questions to consider:

- How was she poor in spirit, or humble, and how did that prepare her for a place of honor?

- Did she mourn the sins of her people? In what ways does she express her grief?

- Meekness is described as strength under control. What strengths do you hear in her message?

- Her passion for righteousness was obvious to all who knew her. She was deeply satisfied with who God is and what He teaches and didn't run after the gods of those around her. How about you?

- She sent a strong message of judgment back to King Josiah. Was there any mercy in her words? How do you know?

- Huldah had a pure heart that abided in the shadow of His Presence. He was her place of safety and security. Read Psalm 91 to see how purity of heart and protection go hand in hand.

- Persecution is certain when we stand for the Lord. Where did Huldah focus her attention in the days of persecution, and how did that prepare her?

7
FERTILITY AND MOTHERHOOD

Fertility—one of the most intimate and vulnerable areas in any woman's life. Should fertility be considered an essential matter for women in all cultures and every generation? Let's explore this topic further as we come to some conclusions together. The definition of essential—**vital, indispensable, important, crucial, critical, and necessary**—provides the basis of our evaluation of the facts regarding fertility and its place in a woman's life. The story of Hannah brings these very facts to life!

You are about to begin a Bible study of a woman named Hannah. This Bible study is designed to help you become familiar with her background, her strengths and weaknesses, and the impact her life had on this world and into the next (her eternal legacy). While I don't want to give away the answers because learning is so much fun, I want to prepare your mind to think critically so that you will live biblically as a result of this study.

What's So Important About Fertility?

So, let's talk about the topic of fertility. My research, although not purely scientific, has convinced me that there is not a woman alive in any culture or generation who has not seriously pondered the essential topic of fertility.

As little girls, most of us want to become mothers one day. Of course, not all of us realize this aspiration. For many, the empty womb can be the greatest source of sorrow and unfulfilled longing that she experiences. When the natural circumstances of life inhibit the ability to have children, some opt for in vitro fertilization. Others choose to adopt. Still others consider a surrogate "womb" to bear their child during pregnancy. And there are women who refocus their attention entirely on bearing spiritual children.

For some women, not having children is a conscious and even happy choice. They feel complete and satisfied without their own biological children. They determine that their fulfillment comes from other essentials in life, such as education, creativity, and even relationships that might otherwise be hindered by the role of mothering. We will talk about the essential role of spiritual motherhood for those who prefer not to have children and for those who simply do not have a choice.

The topic of fertility is a major focus in the Old Testament. From the beginning of creation in the first two chapters of Genesis, the desire of God's heart is for His children to be fruitful and multiply. As I began to research the topic of fertility, I was astounded by the common theme of infertility, starting in the book of Genesis. In some cases, prayer opened the womb of an infertile woman. Some women needed to wait only a short time for their cries to be heard, while others— like Sarah—felt as though their prayers and even God's promise would never be realized. Eventually, through Sarah's womb, and her God-given gift of fertility, the people of God were triumphantly given life, and the Kingdom of God, which from the very beginning was intended to bless *all* nations and *all* peoples, was defined and established (Gen. 12:3).

The New Testament literally begins with a focus on fertility. Here we find the 5 women included in the lineage, or birth line, of our Savior, Jesus Christ, starting with Tamar, then Rahab, Ruth, Bathsheba (mentioned as the widow of Uriah), and Mary (see Matt. 1:3-16). The gift of fertility takes center stage in each of their mysterious and beautiful stories. It then culminates in the Gospel story with the angel's announcement that Mary would be "with child from the Holy Spirit" (Matt. 1:18). Elizabeth, her cousin, would also have a child in her old age—John the Baptist! Ladies, with this as our backdrop, can there be any doubt that fertility is an essential? Heaven came to earth as Mary gave birth to God's Son, our Savior!

While there are other references to fertility and motherhood in the New Testament, there seems to be a subtle shift towards an emphasis on *spiritual mothering*. This shift does not diminish the significance of fertility and motherhood one iota. Rather, it enables us to see through two lenses:

1. our natural inclination towards fertility and the desire to have children
2. our passion to see others born again of the Spirit as we aspire to become spiritual mothers

How beautiful to see through this world, and into the next, through the lens of the Bible! We get a little glimpse of the glory that will be ours when we see Him face to face, "no longer through a glass darkly" (1 Cor. 13:12). We see that this unique gift of mothering is given to women. Starting in the Garden of Eve with the very first woman, we have been given a womb. This life-giving organ of our physical bodies directly correlates with the Life-giving power of God Himself. The New Testament church is characterized by the nurturing care of a mother:

We proved to be gentle among you, as a nursing mother tenderly cares for her own children. Having so a fond affection for you, we were well-pleased to impart to you not only the gospel of God but also our own lives, because you had become very dear to us. 1 Thess. 2:7-8 NASB

What am I saying? Am I saying that God is a woman? Absolutely not.

What I am saying is that we are created in the image of God, both male *and* female, and this mysterious reality makes it clear that God has certain feminine traits that He has endowed the woman with, just as He has given the man specific traits.

Why does this matter? I believe this matters a lot—and here's why. As we fulfill the purpose God has ordained for our lives, we achieve the greatest level of satisfaction possible this side of Heaven. God created and then recreated us to be faithful and fruitful. When we bring a new child into this world through salvation, the Bible says there is great joy in the presence of the angels of God (Luke 15:7, 10). This refers to the joy that God Himself exudes when every single one of His children repents and finds life in Christ! Yes, my friends, we are created in His image. As we can see, as women, we long to bring life into this world and into the next (eternal salvation). Fertility of every kind is closely woven into our very heart and soul!

Spiritual mothering takes place through us as we learn to teach, train, mentor, and minister to the needs of others. We recognize their lives as precious and invaluable.

What are some ways in which you have been involved with spiritual mothering? Have you helped with Vacation Bible School or Backyard Bible Clubs? Have you ministered in a refugee center? How about being available to help your neighbors? Spend some time thinking and sharing what God has done through you and possible dreams you have of being a Life-giving womb to those without Christ.

As we grow in grace, and in years, too, it is wonderful to realize that our lives increase rather than decrease in value as we extend God's love and truth with our words and our actions. We show the love of Christ through our smile and extending acts of kindness and service to those in our community and around the world.

Whether or not you choose to give birth to children, provide foster care, or offer any other form of physical parenting, I pray that you will engage your heart and soul—yes, your body, too—in bringing other souls to salvation through our Lord Jesus Christ. As you read and carefully study the story of Hannah through the lens of inductive Bible study, may you see the transformation that takes place through her longing to give birth to a son—followed by the giving of that very son to the Giver of Life. And may His Life-giving joy be yours in abundance!

> **Sing, O barren one, who did not bear;**
>> **break forth into singing and cry aloud,**
>> **you who have not been in labor!**
> **For the children of the desolate one will be more**
>> **than the children of her who is married," says the LORD.**
> **"Enlarge the place of your tent,**
>> **and let the curtains of your habitations be stretched out;**
> **do not hold back; lengthen your cords**
>> **and strengthen your stakes.**
> **For you will spread abroad to the right and to the left,**
>> **and your offspring will possess the nations**
>> **and will people the desolate cities.** Isa. 54:1-3 ESV

What a promise!

Now, it's your turn. Grab your Bible and notepad, and get ready. God will warm your heart with His love and enlighten your mind with His Truth. You will be transformed as you sit at His feet with a renewed sense of wonder!

Read the story of **Hannah** in 1 Samuel 1-2:1-11, and answer the following questions about the context in which we find her story.

Where do we find her story in the Bible, and who wrote it? When was it written?

The author of 1 Samuel, found in the Old Testament, is unknown, but this passage from 1 Chronicles indicates that Samuel may have written portions of both 1 and 2 Samuel along with Nathan and Gad:

> Now the acts of King David, from first to last, are written in the Chronicles of Samuel, the seer, and in the Chronicles of Nathan the prophet, and in the Chronicles of Gad, the seer, with accounts of all his rule and his might and of the circumstances that came upon him and upon Israel and upon all the kingdoms of the countries. 1 Chron. 29:29-30 ESV

Also, 1 Samuel 10:25 (NASB) states: **"Then Samuel told the people the ordinances of the kingdom and wrote *them* in the book and placed *it* before the LORD. And Samuel sent all the people away, each one to his house."** The book was written approximately 1000 years before Christ was born. It marks Israel's transitional period when the people of Israel began demanding a king like the other nations had, thus becoming a monarchy under Saul, followed by David and finally Solomon.

How does the context inform the meaning of this story?

This story takes place at the conclusion of the period of biblical history recorded in the book of Judges. The very last verse reads: **"In those days there was no king in Israel; everyone did what was right in his own eyes"** (Judg. 21:25 NASB).

No wonder polygamy, which was first noted in Genesis 4:19, was still actively practiced. While it may have been "right in their own eyes," clearly it is not right in the eyes of God who made His desire for faithfulness in marriage quite clear from the first chapter of Genesis. (Sadly, polygamy would be a major factor in Solomon's downfall in the very near future.) At this point in time, however, it was Hannah's daily, present, and painful reality as Peninah, Elkanah's other wife, tormented her at every possible moment.

Infertility was a prominent theme in the Old Testament, starting in the book of Genesis, and it is cited specifically among the patriarchs and their wives, beginning with Sarah (Abraham's wife) and also noted by Rebekah (Isaac's wife) and Rachel (Jacob's wife). The ability to have sons was critical to continuing the family lineage, as a result, infertility was a stigma that was often mistaken as God's displeasure.

All of this sets the stage for the story of Hannah in its original context and provides greater insight for us as we interpret the principles and apply them to our lives even today. History repeats itself unless we learn from it!

We need to pray as we begin, study and research, and prepare to teach others. Why do we make prayer such a significant part of Bible study? What's the big deal about prayer? Remember that this is God's Word, and we need His input every step of the way. As we pray, God will shine His Light on what He wants us to see. He will connect the dots within His Word to cultural norms and individual lives in a way that is highly relevant and deeply personal all at once. He is the God of all wisdom, knowledge, and understanding.

As we transition to the observation phase of the Bible study, we remember the incredible power of prayer. Please join me as we begin the adventure of studying Hannah together.

Dear Lord,

Thank you for the amazing gift of Your Word. Your Word is holy and Life-giving. I pray that you will enable us to embrace the gift of Your Word and all of its treasures as we read and study the story of Hannah through the careful processes of observation, accurate interpretation, fruitful application, and thoughtful reflection together.

Yes! May we apply the timeless truths that we discover about Hannah, fertility. and motherhood in every realm to our lives so that others can see You and Your life beautifully reflected in us.

In Jesus's Name, Amen

The **Observation** window of inductive Bible study answers the question: **"What does the passage say?"**

Read the story of Hannah at least two times. Again, I recommend reading two different translations of the Bible—one that is a word-for-word translation, like the English Standard Version, and one that is thought-for-thought, such as the New International Version. List the chapter and verse where you see the following facts.

It is helpful to read the section of Scripture before and after her story to provide more insight into the context. Avoid consulting study notes in your Bible or reference material until you have completed the observation window. This allows you to have an unfiltered perspective on what God's Word has to say, rather than an opinion of what someone else thinks God's Word has to say.

Who?

1. Make a list of each time Hannah is mentioned in the story, by name or even by pronoun.

_____

_____

_____

_____

_____

_____

_____

_____

_____

2. Make another list of all the people included in her story and how they interacted with one another.

_____

_____

_____

_____

_____

_____

_____

3. Be sure to include a list of all references to God the Father, Jesus Christ, and the Holy Spirit. In addition, take special note of repeated words and phrases. There is a reason why things are listed more than once. Notice how others have forsaken God. What do their actions reveal? Who or what are they worshipping? What does God have to say about the way His people have forsaken Him?

Take special note of repeated words and phrases. I love this quote by Pastor Crawford Loritts: "God does not have a speech impediment. When he repeats himself, he intends to."[29]

_____

_____

_____

_____

_____

_____

_____

[29] Crawford Loritts, "The Call to Courage," Desiring God, February 5, 2008, https://www.desiringgod.org/messages/the-call-to-courage. Accessed October 20, 2020.

Where?

1. Where did Hannah live? Worship? Work? Travel?

_____

_____

_____

_____

_____

2. List all **places** in the story, as well as "where" words like inside, under, and behind that indicate location.

_____

_____

_____

_____

_____

_____

When?

1. When did Hannah live?

_____

_____

_____

_____

_____

_____

2. List all other **time-related words** like "before" or "after," as well as when this takes place in the Bible according to the immediate context.

_____

_____

_____

_____

3. Notice the divine appointments that can only be explained by God Himself.

_____

_____

_____

_____

_____

_____

What?

1. What other important facts do we learn about Hannah?

_____

_____

_____

_____

_____

2. What did Hannah do, say, or contribute?

_____

_____

_____

_____

_____

3. What problem did Hannah create or resolve?

_____

_____

_____

_____

_____

4. What is the single most significant contribution of her life? Her *essential?*

_____

_____

_____

_____

Peter says this about God's promises to us:

> **For by these He has granted to us His precious and magnificent promises, so that by them you may become partakers of the divine nature, having escaped the corruption that is in the world by lust.** 2 Pet. 1:4 NASB

Let's move forward, asking the Holy Spirit to enable us to accurately interpret the Word of God so that we can indeed become "partakers of the divine nature."

Interpretation asks and answers the question: **"What does the story mean?"** Now that we have accurately observed the facts, we can properly interpret and discern the timeless truths that we learn from this biblical account.

In this step, we will list at least two timeless truths from this story (there are usually more than two). The way that we determine if a truth is timeless is by asking: **"Is this true for all people, in all places, and at all times?"**

The following principles and practices of biblical interpretation help us to do just that.

1. **Pray** for wisdom, remembering that the primary purpose of Bible study is to change our lives, not simply to increase our knowledge.
2. **Establish the Bible as *the* authority.** It is the authoritative source of truth, given to us by God Himself (Heb. 4:12; 2 Tim. 3:16-17; Isa. 40:8).
3. **Recognize that the Bible interprets itself**; in other words, Scripture best explains Scripture. Pay attention to the context, cross-references, and repeated words and phrases, along with the type of literature.
4. **Interpret personal experience in the light of Scripture** and *not* Scripture in the light of personal experience. (Syncretism can result from seeing our cultural norms as if they are from God, rather than developing our cultural norms based on God's Word of truth.)
5. **Interpreting a text without context leads to pretext.** Biblical examples are authoritative only when supported by a command. Don't make a command from something that is intended as an illustration, such as Matthew 5:30: **"cut off your right hand."**

Using these principles of interpretation, identify at least two timeless truths that are true for all people, in all places, at all times. Then, list the Bible verses where these truths are found in Esther's story.

Example:

Whichever way God leads, we experience the reality that this God who made us has a wonderful plan for our lives (Jer. 29:11-14). Regardless of the decision we make regarding fertility and motherhood, it is always God's intention that we become spiritual mothers, bringing His life to others!

Timeless Truth #1:
Verse(s):

Timeless Truth #2:
Verse(s):

What Does God Really Say About This?

One woman might pray for children and become pregnant right away, while another woman might pray and wait for years before conceiving. The first woman might assume that she's an example of how God hears and answers prayers according to Matthew 7:7 (NASB), **"Ask, and it will be given to you; seek, and you will find; knock, and it will be opened to you,"** but the second woman might (wrongly) assume that God is neither hearing, nor answering her prayers.

However, the Bible says, **"He has made everything beautiful in its own time"** (Eccles. 3:11 ESV).

There may seem to be a discrepancy between these two Scriptures. In this case, we need to remember the underlying foundational truth of the whole Bible—*God is love*. He is working in ways that we cannot see, hear, nor feel. A prayer that seems to be unanswered today is still being answered. The principle of God's steadfast love and perfect timing is still at work!

Wait on God. Trust in His love. He might rearrange your desires, but He will never fail you!

Application

Application answers the question: **"What does this truth mean for me?"** and **"How do I live in response?"** It is time to apply God's timeless truths to our own lives and to experience the great fulfillment this brings as we move forward into spiritual maturity. This application window helps us to remember what we learn far more than if we only hear or read these truths. It empowers us to both know and do what the Bible says!

And remember, it is a message to obey, not just to listen to. If you do not obey, you are only fooling yourself. For if you just listen and do not obey, it is like looking at your face in a mirror but doing nothing to improve your appearance. You see yourself, walk away, and forget what you look like. But if you keep looking steadily into God's perfect law—and if you do what it says and don't forget what you heard, then God will bless you for doing it. James 1:22-25 NLT

If you are studying this as an individual, read over all the timeless truths you have uncovered. **If you are working with others,** gather in small groups, and read all the timeless truths you have discovered together out loud.

Determine which timeless truth is most relevant for you and other women in your target group. Read and respond to the following questions individually, or ask someone in the group to record your answers. You may only apply one or two of these questions as you develop an application to share, but it's good to review all of them as you prepare.

Ask, "Is there a/an _____?"

1. principle to apply
2. command to obey
3. attitude to change
4. sin to renounce
5. truth to believe
6. example to follow
7. specific action to take

This Bible study method helps you to *remember* and *apply* God's truth to your life—and to multiply that truth into the lives of other women.

If you are studying this Bible study as an individual, prepare a creative way to present your timeless truth through poetry, story, or drama, or reframe it as a current event news article.

If you are studying this as a small group, develop one of the following oral arts to express what you have learned. Create a meaningful:

- song
- dance
- artwork
- skit of a modern life drama from your community and nation
- poetry recitation
- story—yes, tell a story, maybe even *your* story!

Timeless truth to be presented:

_____

Method selected for presentation (song, dance, story, etc.):

_____

If you are studying with other women, each small group will present their application activity before they disclose which timeless truth they have chosen. Ask others what timeless truth they see through the application window.

Reflection

Reflection is our final step, and yet it opens the window of our soul to receive the refreshing wind of the Holy Spirit. Engage in an activity that is refreshing for your soul: prayer, praise, journaling, lamenting, confession, silence, solitude, art, and/or nature appreciation. I like to call these soul food.

These are just a few examples, and others can be discovered and developed by studying Richard Foster's *Celebration of the Disciplines*, or my personal favorite, *The Spirit of the Disciplines* by Dallas Willard.

Simply put, reflection gives us an opportunity for deeper thought and for the Holy Spirit to cleanse us from the inside out. We clean the windows of our soul through contemplative spiritual disciplines and practices. Determine which reflection practice best suits you and this specific study of Hannah's story. Regardless of which method you choose, this is my prayer for you, dear friend, that you may grow in understanding, insight, and love:

> **I pray that from his glorious, unlimited resources, he will empower you with inner strength through his Spirit. Then Christ will make his home in your hearts as you trust in him. Your roots will grow down into God's love and keep you strong. And may you have the power to understand, as all God's people should, how wide, how long, how high, and how deep his love is. May you experience the love of Christ, though it is too great to understand fully. Then you will be made complete with all the fullness of life and power that comes from God.** Eph. 3:16-19, NLT

I am convinced that fertility is an essential for women, even as I am convinced that each woman is born with a physical womb. Regardless of whether we seek to give birth to biological children, adopt a child, or decide that parenting is simply not for us, what we learn from Hannah is even more essential.

We are called to be fruitful, to be spiritual mothers, giving life to others as we introduce them to new life found only in our Lord Jesus Christ. If you have not yet made the choice to receive Him for yourself, may I strongly encourage you to do so? The peace, the joy and the love that He offers is simply out of this world, and yet only available while we are still in this world. Refer to the conclusion to learn more!

Breanna's Story

Strolling along the shore, I spotted a young woman of color, beautifully dressed and holding a bundle of balloons. As I came closer, I noticed that they were birthday balloons. Always ready to celebrate, I joyfully greeted her and asked if it was her birthday. Then I saw it—the bag of ashes that was in her other hand. She replied, "no, it would have been my baby's fourth birthday...."

Breanna (not her real name) and I shared a time of tearful conversation as she told me her story. I asked if I could pray for her, and she enthusiastically replied, "Yes!" She asked me if she could give me a hug. My answer was the same: "Yes, please!" Together we reflected on the beautiful gift of motherhood—and on the power it holds in our lives to bring great joy and an equal measure of sorrow.

As I walked away, I turned to see her releasing the balloons, one by one, towards Heaven. This motherhood moment was a beautiful reflection of the heart of God towards each one of us. It served as a poignant reminder of just how essential the gift of motherhood is to each and every woman, regardless of her personal choices about giving life to biological children.

If you, too, have suffered the deep loss or unfulfilled longings of motherhood, I pray that you will run into the arms of our Savior who loves you with an everlasting love!

8
CREATIVITY THAT LEADS TO GENEROSITY

D O YOU HAVE a creative person in your life? Someone who lives to create? Perhaps your "creative" is a master chef, mixing organic ingredients to create masterpieces that not only delight the eyes but also electrify the taste buds. Maybe your "creative" is a master musician who lives for the moments they come to life at the keyboard or the frets on a guitar. Regardless of their art form, they likely embody several characteristics of a "creative" as defined by the Urban Dictionary:

> A person with a never-ending, intense desire to produce based on originality of thought, expression, etc., that impacts nearly every aspect of their life, both in negative and positive ways.[30]

My mother was a creative. She lived to paint and create. This definition describes her perfectly—she embodied a never-ending, intense, and seemingly insatiable desire to create her next sculpture, watercolor, or oil painting. Mom's creativity blessed many, including me, although it took some years for me to fully

---

[30] "Creative," Urban Dictionary, accessed October 20, 2020, https://www.urbandictionary.com/define.php?term=creative.

understand her artistic passion. When she presented me with a blank piece of paper urging me to create, all I could do was stare at it. We learned to laugh about this in later years.

All too often, creatives are misunderstood as eccentric individuals with lofty ideas; it is often said that "their heads are stuck in the clouds." The truth is that they reflect the pleasure that God Himself enjoys as He dips His brush in the extraordinary palette of Heaven and paints the morning and evening sky; as He uniquely creates each and every snowflake; and as He fills each delicate flower with an intoxicating fragrance. The wonders of His creation astound us, enabling us to experience a tiny portion of His glory through our physical senses. The Message Bible, translated by Eugene Peterson, interprets Galatians 6:1 as: **"Live creatively, friends."**

Peterson expands his thought on this verse in his little daily devotional, *God's Message for Each Day*: "In Christ we are set free to create. He sets us free to live— toward God, with people, in the world—as artists, not as copiers. He sets us free to use the stuff that God gives us to live something original."[31]

When creativity is well developed and artistically displayed it will lead to an abundance in the heart and soul that cannot be easily defined. It must be experienced. The very riches of the Gospel are expressed through creativity. Conversely, when creativity is quenched, the very purposes of God can be thwarted.

Jesus was a creative too. He restored, redeemed, and refined each life He encountered if they let Him. Sadly, people in His own hometown misunderstood and minimized His creative power. Rather, they passed up His words of wisdom and the magnificent miracles they could have received from His hand. In Matthew 13:57-58 (NASB) we read,

And they took offense at him. But Jesus said to them, "A prophet is not without honor except in his hometown and in his own household. And he did not do many mighty works there, because of their unbelief."

The Great Creator, Beautiful Savior, was limited. How astounding. How tragic. And how startling to learn that we, as mere humans, can actually limit His creativity by denying and rejecting His presence in our lives. We can limit one another, too. Rather than recognizing that we are created in His image to do the good and creative

---

[31] Eugene H. Peterson, *God's Message for Each Day, Wisdom from the Word of God* (Nashville, TN: Thomas Nelson Publishing, 2004), 249.

works that He ordained for each of us before the foundation of the world (Eph. 1:4, 2:10), we often pour water on the fire of another person's soul.

Perhaps this is the reason why Lydia, our Bible study subject for the essential of creativity, left her home in Thyatira, Turkey, to resettle and establish what the Bible calls her "household" in Philippi, Greece. Scripture does not reveal the motivation for her move, so we should not presume or proclaim this notion as fact. Even so, the reality of her creativity and the generosity that resulted are clearly evident and beautifully celebrated.

What we do know is that her creative edge made all the difference as she was divinely placed to welcome the Gospel of our Lord Jesus Christ into the western world as a woman of means and purpose. Her creativity led to generosity—the greatest gift of all—the riches of the Gospel brought to untold millions over the centuries.

> **My goal is that they may be encouraged in heart and united in love, so that they may have the full riches of complete understanding, in order that they may know the mystery of God, namely, Christ.** Col. 2:2 NIV

Yes! Creativity is one of God's greatest gifts and one of our essentials. You are about to understand why as we take a journey with this "creative" named Lydia.

> **A (certain) woman named Lydia, from the city of Thyatira, a dealer in purple fabrics who was [already] a worshiper of God, listened to us; and the Lord opened her heart to pay attention and to respond to the things said by Paul. And when she was baptized, along with her household, she pleaded with us, saying, "If you have judged me and decided that I am faithful to the Lord [a true believer], come to my house and stay." And she persuaded us.** Acts 16:14-15 AMP

Preparation

Our first step in this Essentials narrative inductive Bible study is preparation. If you are teaching an *Essentials* Bible study group, or if you are simply studying on your own, here are three simple but vital steps to help you prepare well. Preparation is most definitely an essential. When we prepare a scrumptious recipe, we gather our ingredients, consider the temperature, and then proceed. In much the same way, we prepare for Bible study as we **read, research, and always remember to pray.**

READ her story in an essentially literal Bible translation (word-for-word) such as the English Standard Version and a dynamic equivalent version (thought-for-thought) such as the New Living Translation. Whenever possible, read out loud and more than once.

RESEARCH the background of the story to determine context and the type of literature, and to understand the writer's aim for the original audience. To get you started, I have shared some of my own notes with you below.

REMEMBER TO PRAY—God has something special to say to you through His Word. While the timeless truths in each story are for everyone, He understands you and your needs, and He wants to meet you right where you are. As you pray, you open your heart to receive His personal and practical Word of exhortation and hope.

Although **Lydia's** story doesn't take many words to tell, it is a story that continues to speak volumes of truth to all women until this very day. Read the story of Lydia in Acts 16:11-15 and Acts 16:40.

Where do we find Lydia's story? How does the context inform the meaning?

Acts is a book of history filled with stories, so it is often called historical narrative. We gain a better understanding of her story as we read it in this context. In the fifteenth chapter of Acts, just before her story begins, the leaders of the early Christian church met to determine what part of Jewish Law the new Gentile believers would be required to follow. Interestingly, they call these requirements "essentials," and they include abstaining from meat offered to idols and from sexual immorality in any form. This determination brought great peace to the believers and offered strong encouragement to continue the good work of making disciples in the nations near and far.

According to Acts 15:36, Paul determined that it was time for his second missionary journey to visit the new believers and proclaim the Good News to those who had not yet heard. Read the remainder of Acts 15 through Acts 16:15 in preparation for your inductive study of Lydia.

Who wrote the specific book of the Bible where her story is found, and what do we know about his or her life?

Luke wrote the book of Acts as a continuation of the Gospel of Luke. His purpose for writing is clearly stated in Luke 1:1-4 and Acts 1:1-3. Luke was a physician and an excellent historian. In fact, the book of Acts is considered historical narrative. We are not certain of the date when it was written, but most agree that it was between AD 60 and AD 90, but probably closer to AD 80. Luke traveled with the Apostle Paul and had firsthand knowledge of Paul's life and ministry.

Luke was a Gentile, which gave him a completely different perspective from that of any of the other Gospel writers. In addition, he includes the most accounts of women who encountered Christ and became both disciples and disciple-makers as a result. Lydia is the first of many Gentiles in the western world to believe and follow Christ and to start a church in her own home. The fact that she is a woman does not overshadow the fact that she is a faithful follower of our Lord Jesus Christ, one who offers Him her heart and her home as she makes a way for His Kingdom to come and His will to be done.

Elisabeth Elliot captures the essence of Lydia's contribution in this quote from *Let Me Be a Woman*:

> The fact that I am a woman does not make me a different kind of Christian, but the fact that I am a Christian makes me a different kind of woman.[32]

Yes! We do become a different kind of woman with the love of Christ in our hearts. The prophet Joel pronounced the blessing of restoration in Joel 2:28, "…I will pour out My spirit on all mankind, and your sons and daughters will prophesy". Peter quoted this prophecy on the Day of Pentecost in Acts 2:17-18. Lydia became living proof that God always keeps His promises, including His promises to women. From the beginning of Creation, and throughout history, God intends for men and women to serve Him together.

> **And God created man in His own image, in the image of God He created him; male and female He created them. And God blessed them; and God said to them, "Be fruitful and multiply, and fill the earth, and subdue it; and rule over the fish of the sea and over the birds of the sky, and over every living thing that moves on the earth." And God saw all that He had made, and behold, it was very good.** Gen. 1:27-28, 31a NASB

---

[32] Elisabeth Elliot, *Let Me Be a Woman: Notes to My Daughter on the Meaning of Womanhood* (Wheaton, IL: Living Books, 1988).

I can almost see the angels peering down over the banister of Heaven and applauding the restoration of God's original intention for men and women to serve Him with full dominion and joyful unity!

And now this Good News has been announced to you by those who preached in the power of the Holy Spirit sent from heaven. It is all so wonderful that even the angels are eagerly watching these things happen. 1 Pet. 1:12b NLT

Point to Ponder

"The first effect of the gospel in Europe was a happy harbinger of its emancipation of womanhood by Christianity in striking contrast to paganism and even Judaism."[33]

The New Unger's Bible Handbook

REMEMBER TO PRAY—The statement from Elisabeth Elliot about Lydia sets the stage for the first step of our inductive Bible study process. Before we begin, however, let's remember to pray! First and last, and each step along the way, continue to connect with God in prayer as you study His Word. Remember, we are seated with Him in the heavenlies (Eph. 2:6 NASB), and as we pray, asking for wisdom, insight, and clarity from His Holy Spirit, He pulls back the curtain a bit more to enable us to see what He sees, grow in His grace, and become all that He created us to be!

For we are God's masterpiece. He has created us anew in Christ Jesus, so we can do the good things he planned for us long ago. Eph. 2:10 NLT

Regardless of your ethnic heritage; the color of your eyes, hair, or skin; or your financial position or professional prowess, know this, my dear friend: **God loves you!** You are created in *His image*—you are *His masterpiece*—created *on purpose* and *for His distinct purpose*. As we start discovering Lydia's story, my prayer for you, is that God will illuminate your mind and ignite your heart to further explore your own story!

---

[33] Merrill F. Unger and Gary N. Larson, *The New Unger's Bible Handbook* (Chicago: Moody Press, 1984).

The **Observation** window of inductive Bible study answers the question: **"What does the passage say?"**

Read the story of Lydia at least two times. Again, I recommend reading two different translations of the Bible—one that is a word-for-word translation, like the English Standard Version, and one that is thought-for-thought, such as the New International Version. List the chapter and verse where you see the following facts.

It is helpful to read the section of Scripture before and after her story to provide more insight into the context. Avoid consulting study notes in your Bible or reference material until you have completed the observation window. This allows you to have an unfiltered perspective on what God's Word has to say, rather than an opinion of what someone else thinks God's Word has to say.

Who?

1. Make a list of each time Lydia is mentioned in the story, by name or even by pronoun.

_____

_____

_____

_____

_____

_____

_____

_____

_____

2. Make another list of all the people included in her story and how they interacted with one another.

   For example: How did Lydia interact with Paul and his traveling companions? What do we learn about her personality? Her work style? How might this have been influenced by her creativity and the way she learned to market her creative wares?

_____

_____

_____

_____

_____

_____

_____

3. Be sure to include a list of all references to God the Father, Jesus Christ, and the Holy Spirit. Be sure to reference the way God prepared Paul to travel to Philippi in Acts 16:6-13 and the way in which God is uniquely identified in verse 7.

_____

_____

_____

_____

_____

_____

_____

_____

Who did God send to speak to Paul in verse 9?

_____

_____

_____

_____

_____

Notice how Lydia is described as a "God-fearer" or "worshiper of God" in verse 14. What does that mean? How did that impact her response and the response of others in her circle of influence? What do their actions reveal?

_____

_____

_____

_____

_____

_____

Where?

1. Where did Lydia live? Worship? Work? Travel?

_____

_____

_____

_____

_____

2. List all **places** in the story, as well as "where" words like inside, under, and behind that indicate location.

_____

_____

_____

_____

_____

_____

_____

_____

3. Where did they find Lydia? Why is that significant?

_____

_____

_____

_____

_____

_____

_____

_____

_____

This is an illustration[34] of the Ignatian Way (via Egnatia) which was both a trade route and a road for the soldiers who came to conquer most of the known world at the time for the Roman Empire. What access did this road provide for the Gospel?

When?

1. When did Lydia live?

_____

_____

_____

_____

_____

_____

[34] From: Louis Werner and Photography and video by Matthieu Paley, "Via Egnatia to Rome and Byzantium," accessed November 11, 2020, https://www.aramcoworld.com/Articles/July-2015/Via-Egnatia-to-Rome-and-Byzantium.

2. List all other **time-related words** like "before" or "after," as well as when this take place in the Bible according to the immediate context.

_____

_____

_____

_____

3. Notice the divine appointments that can only be explained by God Himself.

_____

_____

_____

_____

_____

What?

1. What other important facts do we learn about Lydia?

_____

_____

_____

_____

2. What did Lydia do, say, or contribute?

_____

_____

_____

_____

3. What problem did Lydia create or resolve?

_____

_____

_____

_____

_____

_____

4. What is the single most significant contribution of her life? Her *essential*?

_____

_____

_____

_____

_____

Lydia's story was radically changed that day by the river. Her entire life seems to have been a preparation for this divine appointment. I wonder what she thought about that morning as she prepared to gather with the other women for prayer. I wonder if she somehow knew that this was a day like no other in her story. I wonder, don't you?

By now, I hope you have a fresh perspective on what the Holy Spirit is saying to *you*, and how this story, and the truths within it, will impact your life. If you complete the observation of her story, and still have unanswered questions, then consult resources such as the notes in your study Bible, dictionaries, and commentaries, etc.

Peter says this about God's promises to us:

> **For by these He has granted to us His precious and magnificent promises, so that by them you may become partakers of the divine nature, having escaped the corruption that is in the world by lust.** 2 Pet. 1:4 NASB

Let's move forward, asking the Holy Spirit to enable us to accurately interpret the Word of God so that we can indeed become "partakers of the divine nature."

3 Interpretation

Interpretation asks and answers the question: **"What does the story mean?"** Now that we have accurately observed the facts, we can properly interpret and discern the timeless truths that we learn from this biblical account.

In this step, we will list at least two timeless truths from this story (there are usually more than two). The way that we determine if a truth is timeless is by asking: **"Is this true for all people, in all places, and at all times?"**

The following principles and practices of biblical interpretation help us to do just that.

1. **Pray** for wisdom, remembering that the primary purpose of Bible study is to change our lives, not simply to increase our knowledge.
2. **Establish the Bible as *the* authority.** It is the authoritative source of truth, given to us by God Himself (Heb. 4:12; 2 Tim. 3:16-17; Isa. 40:8).
3. **Recognize that the Bible interprets itself**; in other words, Scripture best explains Scripture. Pay attention to the context, cross-references, and repeated words and phrases, along with the type of literature.
4. **Interpret personal experience in the light of Scripture** and *not* Scripture in the light of personal experience. (Syncretism can result from seeing our cultural norms as if they are from God, rather than developing our cultural norms based on God's Word of truth.)
5. **Interpreting a text without context leads to pretext**. Biblical examples are authoritative only when supported by a command. Don't make a command from something that is intended as an illustration, such as Matthew 5:30: **"cut off your right hand."**

Example:

Creativity plus hard work prepare us for generous acts of service. **"She opens her hand to the poor and reaches out her hand to the needy"** (Prov. 31:20 ESV).

Using these principles of interpretation, identify at least two timeless truths that are true for all people, in all places, at all times. Then, list the Bible verses where these truths are found in Esther's story.

Timeless Truth #1:
Verse(s):

Timeless Truth #2:
Verse(s):

What Does God Say About This?

When we wait on God, He works on our behalf, turning our prison into a pathway of victory as we choose to praise Him in that place. We see this illustrated in both of these amazing Old and New Testament accounts:

And when they began singing and praising, the LORD set ambushes against the sons of Ammon, Moab, and Mount Seir ... and they were struck down. 2 Chron. 20:22 NASB (full account: 2 Chron. 20:14-25)

About midnight Paul and Silas were praying and singing hymns of praise to God, and the prisoners were listening to them and suddenly there came a great earthquake... Acts 16:25-26 NASB (full account: Acts 16:25-33)

Application

> **Application** answers the question: **"What does this truth mean for me?"** and **"How do I live in response?"** It is time to apply God's timeless truths to our own lives and to experience the great fulfillment this brings as we move forward into spiritual maturity. This application window helps us to remember what we learn far more than if we only hear or read these truths. It empowers us to both know and do what the Bible says!
>
> **And remember, it is a message to obey, not just to listen to. If you do not obey, you are only fooling yourself. For if you just listen and do not obey, it is like looking at your face in a mirror but doing nothing to improve your appearance. You see yourself, walk away, and forget what you look like. But if you keep looking steadily into God's perfect law—and if you do what it says and don't forget what you heard, then God will bless you for doing it.** James 1:22-25 NLT

If you are studying this as an individual, read over all the timeless truths you have uncovered. **If you are working with others,** gather in small groups, and read all the timeless truths you have discovered together out loud.

Determine which timeless truth is most relevant for you and other women in your target group. Read and respond to the following questions individually, or ask someone in the group to record your answers. You may only apply one or two of these questions as you develop an application to share, but it's good to review all of them as you prepare.

Ask, "Is there a/an _____?"

1. principle to apply
2. command to obey
3. attitude to change
4. sin to renounce
5. truth to believe
6. example to follow
7. specific action to take

This Bible study method helps you to *remember* and *apply* God's truth to your life—and to multiply that truth into the lives of other women.

If you are studying this Bible study as an individual, prepare a creative way to present your timeless truth through poetry, story, or drama, or reframe it as a current event news article.

If you are studying this as a small group, develop one of the following oral arts to express what you have learned. Create a meaningful:

- song
- dance
- artwork
- skit of a modern life drama from your community and nation
- poetry recitation
- story—yes, tell a story, maybe even *your* story!

Timeless truth to be presented:

_____

Method selected for presentation (song, dance, story, etc.):

_____

If you are studying with other women, each small group will present their application activity before they disclose which timeless truth they have chosen. Ask others what timeless truth they see through the application window.

Reflection is our final step, and yet it opens the window of our soul to receive the refreshing wind of the Holy Spirit. Engage in an activity that is refreshing for your soul: prayer, praise, journaling, lamenting, confession, silence, solitude, art, and/or nature appreciation. I like to call these soul food.

These are just a few examples, and others can be discovered and developed by studying Richard Foster's *Celebration of the Disciplines*, or my personal favorite, *The Spirit of the Disciplines* by Dallas Willard.

Spend some time reflecting on what you have just discovered from the life of Lydia. Reflection is a key component of spiritual transformation. There is a profound difference between seeking information and transformation. The former results in increased knowledge; the latter results in a heart that is changed and a life that reflects the loving purposes of our God.

As a reminder, a few of the spiritual practices that you might enjoy as you study individual women, or even groups of women, in the Bible include:

- *Lectio Divina*, or personal meditation on the Word of God
- solitude
- silence
- fasting
- fellowship
- confession
- creativity

I invite you to look out the **window of reflection** through Lydia's story. Ask yourself how creativity may have helped her through years of waiting. Ponder the process of moving from one nation to another as a single businesswoman.

What were her innermost desires that she shared with God and with the other women in her circle as they gathered at the river to pray each week on their day of rest and worship, the Sabbath?

Undoubtedly, she knew that the God of Israel is a God who hears and answers prayer as revealed through His prophets. **"Call to Me and I will answer you, and I will tell you great and mighty things, which you do not know"** (Jer. 33:3 NASB). Did she have a journal where she recorded her prayers, waiting for His reply? Little did she know that God heard all of her prayers and was just about to answer!

According to Diana Curren Bennett, "a journal is like a spiritual diary . . . to reflect on our state of soul, our various moods and their implications, our personal disciplines or lack thereof, our failures, celebrations, concerns, sins, prayers and yearnings."[35] I wholeheartedly agree. Journaling is a lifeline for me and something I practice each and every day as I greet the morning, and the Lord who made that morning, in order to center my soul's desires in Him. My journal is a safe place to bring my requests to Him and then wait with keen expectation:

Listen to my voice in the morning, LORD. Each morning I bring my requests to you and wait expectantly. Ps. 5:3 NLT

Journaling is an exercise in both speaking to God, through the words that we write, and in listening for His reply, as expressed here by the psalmist. Again, this is consistent with the Bible; we see examples of this in both the Old and New Testaments. Jesus frequently asked people to express what they both wanted and needed. Here are a few examples:

- **"What are you looking for?"** Jesus asked two of John's disciples in John 1:35-41.
- **"What do you want?"** Jesus asked the mother of the sons of Zebedee in Matthew 20:20-28.
- **"What do you want me to do for you?"** Jesus asked the two blind men in Matthew 20:29-34 as He was moved to compassion.
- **"Do you want to be made well?"** Jesus asked the invalid who lay by the pool of Beth-zatha in John 5:2-9. This man had been lying there for 38 years. Perhaps all of those years of waiting were a prison, and Jesus was just about to release this man into his own personal pathway of victory!

Ruth Haley Barton has this to say about expressing expectation and desire to Christ in prayer:

> Sometimes, as we pay attention to our desire, we are made aware that there are choices for us to make. Jesus's question to the paralyzed man at the pool of Beth-zatha, "Do you want to be made well?" (John 5:6), called for him to take some sort of movement in the direction of his desire. Getting in touch with how badly he wanted healing and his

---

[35] Diana Curren Bennett, "The Journal," *SILENCIO - LEADERSHIP TRANSFORMATIONS*, June 2020, https://www.leadershiptransformations.org/documents/Silencio.pdf.

willingness to do what he could catalyzed Jesus's power to do the one thing he could not do for himself.[36]

Strongly consider journaling as your final step in your study of Lydia. I recommend buying an inexpensive journal to share your matters of the heart, concerns, and desires with God—and God alone. If possible, write a page as you begin each day by reading His Word, writing out your requests and the response God brings through His Word and His Spirit.

I am confident that you will be blessed as you do this. As you return and revisit your journal in the days ahead, you will see firsthand that Jesus's compassion for you in the midst of your desire is real. He will enable you to embrace what is good and remove what is destructive. And, just like Lydia, you will experience and embrace creativity that leads to generosity.

Yes! Lydia and her creative edge made all the difference, as she was divinely placed to welcome the Gospel of our Lord Jesus Christ into the western world as a woman of means and purpose. Her creativity led to generosity—the greatest gift of all—the riches of the Gospel brought to untold millions over the centuries.

Dear friend,

Have you put your trust in Christ alone to save you from your sin? You may be highly creative and extremely generous, too. But until and unless you place your trust in Christ, you have no assurance of your eternal destiny. Let today be the day that, just like Lydia, you bring all that you have and all that you need before Him with prayer and confident expectation!

He promises that, **"whoever comes to Me, I will never cast out"** (John 6:37 ESV). **"But to all who receive Him, who believed in His name, He gave the right to become children of God"** (John 1:12 ESV).

The conclusion of this matter, ***His Essential Love for You***, helps us to do just that.

---

[36] R. Ruth Barton, *Life Together in Christ: Experiencing Transformation in Community* (Downers Grove: IVP Books, an imprint of InterVarsity Press, 2014).

CONCLUSION
His Essential Love for You

The LORD appeared to me from far away.
I have loved you with an everlasting love;
therefore I have continued my faithfulness to you.
Jer. 31:3 ESV

God loves you deeply and wants to share life in His Son and His Holy Spirit with you in intimate and Life-giving ways. The way to receive this life in Christ is pure, and yet it's very powerful. Follow along step-by-step, and you will discover this for yourself. Here are some essential truths that each of us needs to recognize in order to receive His essential love and plan for our life:

- God loves you and has a wonderful plan for your life.
- Sin separates each and every person from God, His love, and His plan.
- God is not willing that any should perish apart from Him but wants all to come to repentance. Jesus said to Nicodemus, "you must be born again." We read in John 1:12 (NASB), **"But as many as received Him, to them He gave the right to become children of God, even to those who believe in His name."**
- The wages, or what we earn and deserve, of our sin is death, but the free gift of God is eternal life in Christ Jesus our Lord (Rom. 6:23).

Would you like to receive the free gift of abundant and eternal life right now? God is waiting for you to call out to Him. He invites you to follow these simple next steps:

1. Admit your need and desire to know Christ as Savior.
2. Be willing to turn from your sin (anything that separates you from God's love and truth).
3. Trust that Jesus Christ died for you on the cross and rose from the grave to provide forgiveness and to open the way for you to know Him freely and fully.
4. Invite Jesus Christ to come into your life and lead you in a new relationship with God. (This is what it means to be "born again" and receive new life!)

Dear God,

Thank You for Your infinite love for me. I acknowledge that I am a sinner and need Your salvation. I believe that You, Jesus, died for my sins and rose from the grave to overcome the power of sin. Please come into my life and be my Savior. I place my trust in You alone to save me. Teach me to follow You one day at a time, from this day onward.

In Jesus's Name, Amen

His Word promises that, **"…if you confess with your mouth Jesus as Lord, and believe in your heart that God raised Him from the dead, you will be saved"** (Rom. 10:9 NASB).

And that is just the beginning!

As you begin to grow in relationship with Him, His life will grow in you, filling every aspect of your life and transforming the way you think, feel, and live. Your life will then overflow into the lives of others, so that they can have life too!

Jesus said that if we bring our thirst to Him, He will not only quench it, but we will become a fountain of Life-giving power to those around us:

> **"If anyone thirsts, let him come to me and drink.**
> **Rivers of living water will brim and spill out of the depths**
> **of anyone who believes in me this way,**
> **just as the Scripture says."**
>
> John 7:37-38 MSG

EPILOGUE
One Thing Only Is Essential

His very presence brought her to her knees. She hung on every word. Never before did a man

> *teach like He did,*
>
> > *live like He did,*
> >
> > > *help like He did,*
> > >
> > > > *care like He did.*

Never before did a man, a religious man at that, include women in His inner circle and not only allow, but also strongly encourage, them to follow closely as His disciples.

But, ah, this was no ordinary man.

This was the *Son of Man*, the very Son of God, our Savior and Lord. Jesus the Christ.

Mary of Bethany was seated at His feet listening to the Lord's Word. Jesus had this to say about both her posture and priority:

> **"Mary, who sat before the Master, hanging on every word he said. . . One thing _only_ is essential and Mary has chosen it—it's the main course, and won't be taken from her."** Luke 10:39,42 MSG (emphasis mine)

> **"Mary, who moreover <u>was listening</u> to the Lord's word, seated at His feet . . .only a few things are necessary, really only one, for Mary has chosen the good part, which shall not be taken from her."** Luke 10:39,42 NASB (emphasis mine)

The word used for "listening" in Luke 10:39 is translated from the Greek word *akouo*, and literally means to give audience, to hear effectually with our inner ear of the mind, to understand, and to seek to obey.[37] She was rewarded with words of pure commendation from God Himself, and with a promise—*"the good part which shall not be taken from her."* We don't know the rest of Mary's story here on earth, but we can be certain that as long as she continued to listen and obey, she continued to find rest at His feet.

---

[37] James Strong and Spiros Zodhiates, *The Hebrew-Greek Key Study Bible: New American Standard Bible* (Chattanooga, TN: AMG Publishers, 1994).

Yes, Mary discovered the essential for a meaningful life and an eternal legacy, and her eternal legacy continues, leading many to do the same—including me and you—connecting us as women across cultures and generations.

Some 2,000 years later, we continue to learn from Mary's story and rejoice in her example as a woman who

> *listened intently to the Word of God,*
>
> *hung on His every word,*
>
> *joyfully obeyed, knowing that obedience brings blessing.*

The promises of God are realized as we listen, obey, and tell others.

As we conclude this book, *Essentials*, this is my earnest prayer for you! I greatly desire that you learn how to **prepare, observe, interpret, apply, and then reflect**—listening for the Master's voice to speak to you in beautifully intimate ways that only you will comprehend.

God longs to speak and fellowship with you just as He did with Adam and Eve in the Garden of Eden. Sadly, in their sin, they hid from His Holy Presence. Don't hide! Run into His arms, rest in the shade of His love, and feast on the "main course" of His Life-giving Word.

Ponder God's Word in all of its depth, breadth, and beauty. Swim freely in the ocean of His love, and drink deeply to satisfy every longing of your soul and spirit. Allow His Word to transform you from the inside out, from glory to glory.

We invite you to continue the conversation at our *Essentials* blog found on our Women in the Window International website:

www.womeninthewindow-intl.org/essentials

(The Companion Study Guide for *Essentials* will be released in 2021.)

As we connect women with one another across cultures and generations, we hope that will include *you*!

Together, we will continually choose the posture and priority of Mary, confident that we have in fact found the One and only thing that is *essential*—and it won't be taken from us, not now, *not ever*.

PHOTO CREDITS

Chapter 2

Wardrobe
Photo by: Pixel-Shot/Shutterstock.com

Chapter 3

Right-Facing Praying Woman
Photo by: Ben White/Unsplash.com

Woman With Microscope
Photo by: H_Ko/Shutterstock.com

Hands on Bible
Photo by: Kelly Sikkema/Unsplash.com

Woman in Mirror
Photo by: Taylor Smith/Unsplash.com

Woman Looking up Outside
Photo by: Ben White/Unsplash.com

Chapter 4

Couple Walking on Train Tracks
Heng Films/Unsplash.com

Five Friends
pixelheadphoto digitalskillet/Shutterstock.com

Chapter 5

Woman With Headscarf
Boiko Olha/Shutterstock.com

Chapter 6

Female Student in the City
Michaelpuche/Shutterstock

Chapter 7

Mother and Baby
Syda Productions/Shutterstock.com

Chapter 8

Seamstress at Her Work
S_L/Shutterstock.com

Back Cover Author Photo

Andrea Graeve/Photography & Design

All other photos belong to the author

ACKNOWLEDGMENTS

"The Moving Finger writes; and, having writ, Moves on. . ."
—Omar Khayyám

For as long as I can remember, I've loved to read. I have especially loved reading books about women who left an indelible mark on this world in spite of great peril and against all odds. Helen Keller, Marie Curie, even Joan of Arc caught my fancy as a young girl. I was much more likely to be found voraciously reading a biography than a Nancy Drew novel. My extraordinary high school English teacher, Mrs. Rachel Perry Jerry, had a profound impact on my love for reading. She was the first to expand my scope to include writing. With fearful trepidation, I stuck my toe in the water of writing and enthusiastically completed every assignment this dignified teacher gave me. She had a way of making you want to complete anything and everything she asked, with absolute excellence.

You can imagine my delight when (some 20 years later) I discovered that the Bible contains biographies of more than 100 women and girls. While their stories might not be told in their entirety, we catch a beautiful glimpse of their joys, sorrows, and struggles. As I learned to study them inductively through the lens of Precept Ministries International at the feet of Kay Arthur, and to include activity that engages all the senses through the phenomenal teaching of Dr. Howard Hendricks, their stories came to life before my eyes.

Finally, it was the "windows" of Dave Veerman's *How to Apply the Bible*[38] that equipped and empowered me to share this discovery with women around the world through the Women in the Window (narrative inductive) Bible study method. First stop: Ubon Ratchatani Province, Thailand on the shore of the Mekong River, bordering Laos. First audience: 65 women from the Isaan people group, hungry to learn and grow in the grace and knowledge of our Lord and Savior, Jesus Christ. But it was their enthusiastic application using the oral arts of drama, song, dance, and storytelling that brought it all together, breathing His Life into our very souls.

I want to offer my deepest gratitude to Kay Arthur, Dr. Howard Hendricks, Dave Veerman, and, yes, Mrs. Rachel Perry Jerry. But perhaps the greatest debt of gratitude is owed to the hundreds of women across Africa, Asia, and the Middle East who continue to be God's instruments of grace to instruct and teach me in the way that I should go. Most recently, it was Nada, Kiki, and Basma, women leaders in the Middle East, who strongly encouraged me to focus on that which matters most to every woman in every nation and generation.

Yet, without the help of my publisher and editor, Bonnie Lyn Smith of Ground Truth Press, this would remain an incomplete project rather than the book you now hold in your hands. She has faithfully handled each page and every word to enable us to benefit from the way God's moving Finger writes our stories in the indelible sand of both time and eternity.

May His story continue to be told in and through your own.

---

[38] David Veerman, *How to Apply the Bible: Discover the Truths of Scripture and Put Them into Practice* (Place of publication not identified: Livingston Corporation, 2009).

ESSENTIALS

Above all, in all and through all, I acknowledge the Lord and His Word as the only Source of all Truth, and like the Preacher in Ecclesiastes as I sought to **"find delightful words and to write words of truth correctly"** (Eccles. 12:10 NASB).

ABOUT THE AUTHOR

Kim Kerr is no stranger to working across cultures and generations. She has served women around the world for more than 20 years, traveling to 44 nations. She is the mother of four grown children and the grandmother of eleven. Her own journey has taught her to seek and find life's essentials from the Word of God—as well as a deep, abiding relationship with the God of the Word.

In *Essentials*, communicating with both wisdom and passion, Kim shares how to live a life that is deeply fulfilling and empowering, encouraging us to become a beacon of hope and help for our fellow travelers.

As the Executive and Founding Director of Women in the Window International, as well as Mom and "Mimi," she inspires others to find their own story within His— and to live a life that counts for both now and eternity.

If you appreciated **Essentials**,
kindly consider leaving a review at *Amazon* or *Goodreads*.

More resources to this *Essentials* Bible study can be found at:
www.womeninthewindow-intl.org/essentials

The Companion Study Guide for *Essentials* will be released in 2021.

Women in the Window International

Equipping and Empowering Women in the 10/40 Window and beyond to replace poverty and injustice with dignity and purpose in Christ.

Women in the Window International is part of a collaborative movement to equip and empower women leaders, who in turn equip and empower other women leaders. Our focus is on development rather than on relief.

Women in the Window International provides comprehensive training for women in their unique context and culture so that local women leaders are equipped to train other women to fulfill their God-given potential. We do so as part of our vibrant relationships and ongoing partnerships with indigenous, locally-led ministries in Africa, Asia, America and the Middle East.

In addition, we participate in collaborative and creative networks of Christian ministry established in some of the most difficult places on earth for the Gospel to spread. Yet, because of the training, we see women become life-changing and transformational agents of Christ's love and power within their homes, churches, communities, nations, and beyond, as some serve across national boundaries and overcome barriers that we may never be able to overcome.

Women in the Window International is a 501c3 nonprofit organization and an accredited member of the Evangelical Council of Financial Accountability (ECFA).

Women in the Window International
2101 Vista Parkway, Suite 253
West Palm Beach, FL 33411
561-249-5377

Want to know how you can be involved? Contact us!

info@womeninthewindow-intl.org
https://womeninthewindow-intl.org

Made in the USA
Columbia, SC
27 December 2020